The Heart Has Sea

GRAHAM DOWELL

‘The Heart has Seasons . . .’

Travelling Through The Christian Year

CHURCHMAN PUBLISHING
1989

'The Heart has Seasons . . .'
by
Graham Dowell
was first published in 1989 by
Churchman Publishing Limited
117 Broomfield Avenue
Worthing, West Sussex BN14 7SF

Publisher: Peter Smith

Represented in
Dublin; Sydney; Wellington;
Kingston, Ontario and Wilton, Connecticut

Distributed to the book trade by
Bailey Book Distribution Limited
(a division of the Bailey and Swinfen Holdings Group)
Warner House, Wear Bay Road
Folkestone, Kent CT19 6PH

ISBN 1 85093 124 0

Book production by C.M.D. Ltd, Bournemouth.

Contents

Four seasons fill the measure of the year;
  There are four seasons in the mind of man:
He has his lusty Spring, when fancy clear
  Takes in all beauty with an easy span:
He has his Summer, when luxuriously
  Spring's honied cud of youthful thought he loves
To ruminate, and by such dreaming nigh
  His nearest unto heaven: quiet coves
His soul has in its Autumn, when his wings
  He furleth close; contented so to look
On mists in idleness – to let fair things
  Pass by unheeded as a threshold brook.
He has his Winter too of pale misfeature,
  Or else he would forego his mortal nature.

John Keats

Dedication

To my family
near and extended
who have taught me
all I know
and much I have forgotten
– with love

A Note on Language

I am aware that I have offended against the principles of 'inclusive language' and beg the indulgence of those who rightly object that 'him' does not necessarily include 'her'.

I need hardly say that when I refer to God, for instance, as '*He* Who Is' I in no sense wish to imply *maleness*. It is simply that our language has not kept pace with our sensibilities. He/She or (s)he is clumsy and distracting – how much more fortunate the Hebrews who could cheerfully use a plural, Elohim, thus avoiding the difficulty!

The Illustrations

I am deeply grateful to *Ann Clark* for her drawings which bring to the text a magic – a kind of visible music – which mere words cannot convey.

G.D.

1

Introductory

The best teachers agree that if you want to learn a skill or a discipline you must start not from where you would like to be, but from where you are: who you are and what you have been given. Proverbial wisdom bears this out with sayings like: 'The road to Samarkand starts from your front door'; 'The journey of a thousand miles begins with a single step'.

If, unlike the vast majority in this or any other age, I have the power and privilege of choice and so can travel hopefully, I may be able to choose my goal, the desired point of arrival. However I cannot choose the starting-point, where I am now. This, the present moment, the first day of the rest of my life, is the fixed point to which all else is related – the route taken, the fellow-travellers, the luggage and the mode of transport.

My present fixed point is a small and beautiful town on the Welsh–Shropshire border. The border is a good place to be, with all its opportunities to cross the cultures and make foraging expeditions. Anyone who has exchanged, as we have, a metropolitan for a rural way of life confronts almost for the first time the hard reality of Seasons. City-dwellers may notice, with delight or annoyance, seasonal change; but unless they are homeless, on the bread-line, elderly or infirm, they carry on regardless for most of the time. To be suburban is to have no fixed boundaries in space or time. Town and country are inextricably intertwined, Spring melts almost imperceptibly into Summer and only the Guys and bonfires mark the dying of Autumn and the approach of Winter.

In the countryside, on the other hand, seasons still govern your life. You are aware of the subtle changes, hints of growth, decay and transformation obscured by suburbia. You are surprised and a little alarmed by the powerful impenetrability of darkness, without the insistent presence of street-lighting, neon signs and moving traffic. Night and day, summer and winter, are no longer blurred and indistinct; they have discovered clear outlines and recognisable boundaries.

But there are also seasons of the human spirit which penetrate more deeply than the weather and dictate not just the day to day ordering of life but our attitudes to life itself. We carry the seasons within us as well as experiencing them around us and can readily respond to images that reflect them. We can all recognise what Shakespeare meant by 'the winter of our discontent', and many a lover has thought (even if he has not actually said to the beloved): 'Thine eternal summer shall not fade'.

> Four seasons fill the measure of the year;
> There are four seasons in the mind of man,

says Keats – and also, we would add, in spirit and the very bones.

To recognise that moods, attitudes, even beliefs are 'seasonal' gives grounds for hope as well as a cautionary warning. This summer I love and warm to can never, of course, be 'eternal': shall I still love the autumn that succeeds it? The winter that seems utterly boring and hopeless will in fact be succeeded by a spring that will at least dilute my discontent with the promise of new life and fresh possibilities. The old jingle: 'If winter comes, will spring be far behind?' has its own message of hope for those whose clouds seem to have no silver linings and for whom no light is visible at the end of the tunnel.

To be deprived of such boundaries is to risk the Slough of Despond or the Ivory Tower of Complacency. Psychologists and sociologists have warned us that without them we lose identity or become victims of 'anomie'. It is the state of mind which the mediaeval writers called 'accidie' and the Psalmist described as 'the sickness that destroyeth in the noonday', when the desert stretches endlessly, tracklessly ahead. We need markers, symbols to help us recognise where we are and what we are about: what progress has been made and how far there is still to go. We need stages to denote growth, *rites de passage* from birth through puberty and marriage to ageing, retirement and death. Without them we flounder in a suburban morass of seasonless mediocrity.

We have, however, been thrown a lifeline, maps and compasses; we have inherited a network of symbols, markers of change, growth and development. We have inherited the many-splendoured mosaic of the Christian Year. Other believers, like the Jewish community, have their own markers, some of even longer standing and greater durability even than our own. They have helped them survive their historical catastrophes and endless succession of pogroms, periods of exile and Diaspora, from Babylon to Buchenwald, More than anything except, perhaps, the sense of a unique destiny and the overpowering 'shekinah' that has accompanied them, like that pillar of cloud, down the centuries, these symbols have given the Jewish people an identity. And that identity has conferred self-image and self-worth and marks them out as par excellence the 'peculiar people'.

Mary Douglas has described the loss of such markers for the Irish community in England when the rule of Friday abstinence was relaxed by the Catholic hierarchy and replaced by the freedom to choose a personal way of self-denial. The Friday fast points to Calvary and Redemption as clearly as Ramadhan points to Mecca and helps to define the Islamic community. 'At its lowest,' says Mary Douglas, 'it means what haggis and pipes mean to Scots abroad on Burns night. At its most it means what abstaining from pork meant to the Venerable Eleazar as narrated in 2 Maccabees . . . Symbols are the only means of communication. They are the only means of expressing value; the main instruments of thought, the only regulators of experience.'[1] She likens the removal of such valuable non-verbal symbols to manning liturgical signal-boxes with colour-blind signalmen!

It may have been important to correct what had widely become a merely formal observance of the Friday fast and stress the internal attitude rather than the external act. The danger lay in transforming a living link with Calvary, the means of grace and the hope of glory, into yet another opportunity to give to CAFOD and support the church in the Third World. Moreover, what has happened to Friday may also happen to that central symbol of all Christians, the observance of the Eucharist. Here, too, the underlying intention to internalise, to emphasise Word/Edification rather than Action/Transformation, may devalue the symbolic in the interests of the therapeutic. The hungry sheep look up for metaphysics and are given morals.

'There is no person', warns Mary Douglas, 'whose life does not need to unfold in a coherent symbolic system. The less organised the way of life, the less articulated the symbolic system may be.

But social responsibility is no substitute for symbolic forms and indeed depends on them. When ritualism is openly despised the philanthropic impulse is in danger of defeating itself. For it is an illusion to suppose that there can be organisation without symbolic expression . . . Those who despise ritual, even at its most magical, are cherishing in the name of reason a very irrational concept of communication.'[2]

What is true of ritual and liturgy is true also of the 'liturgical year'. What could mean, in secular, linear terms, one dreary day after another, 'tomorrow and tomorrow and tomorrow . . . ', takes on shape and form, movement and rhythm, since time itself needs redeeming and the seasons of the year have to find their own resonances in the seasons of the spirit. There seems little point in arguing whether or not Christ should be born in midwinter and then die and rise again in the spring. Certainly for no historical reason! However socially useful in providing (at least for Western Europeans) a time for celebration, Saturnalia, bread and circuses, at a conveniently dark and traditionally gloomy time of year: however anthropologically right it is to celebrate the dying and rising god at a season of new lambs and new crops: however well we have been conditioned to think in this way of our central festivals, it is undeniable that those resonances are widely felt and deeply experienced.

No one, however secular, can happily contemplate an endless desert of days without the punctuation of oases to refresh and fortify the traveller. Every week must have its Sabbath, even if it be used for fishing, sleeping, News of the World and Songs of Praise. However Brave (or bleak) the New World coming, it will need, as communist regimes well know, its National Heroes' Days to raise our sights and give significance to the rest of the year. This sacramental principle, whereby the special sanctifies the ordinary, outlasts the performance of any purely sacramental acts. If without vision the people perish, it is the cycle of the year, liturgical or not, which lends that vision its focus and perspective. Without it our lives become a mere sentence, a succession of words without meaning.

It is one of the saddest features of long-term unemployment that for many some of the most familiar reference-points have disappeared. Instead of the established ritual of clocking in and out, Monday to Friday, catching the necessary bus, being an invaluable, even necessary member of a team or process, there is nothing to give shape to the week. What may have seemed at times a wearisome treadmill now seems in retrospect the factor above all others that conveyed self-respect, conferred identity and gave meaning and purpose to one's life.

The 'Faith in the City' Report emphasised the erosion of self-respect, the sense of hopelessness, apathy and impotence that is no small part of the misery of unemployment.[3] A similar loss of identity is experienced under the impact of divorce, bereavement or acute disablement. The loss of a life-partner may well mean the loss of the role as well as the status formerly conferred by that partner. When accompanied by the loss of the family house and the supportive community, as in the case of the bereaved clergy wife or the wife of a General Practitioner, for example, this can cause acute anguish and possible breakdown. It is when these familiar props and buttresses have been lost that we look around for other belief- and value-systems that give meaning and purpose to our lives.

Some people can only believe when the going is good, 'God's in his heaven, all's right with the world.' For them, fair-weather faith crumbles when the going is hard and the elements hostile. Others, called by Albert Camus 'winter Christians', actually find faith in adversity: when the pain is most poignant, the issue uncertain, and they are driven to think through the grounds of belief more deeply. At that point it becomes more, not less necessary to believe. It is a constant source of amazement that the very same conditions seem to serve to encourage belief in some and extinguish it in others. Awareness of the power of evil in the world makes faith impossible for some but essential for others. What broke the faith of many in the two World Wars brought a philosopher like C.E.M. Joad back to faith. He examined all the options and decided that Christianity was the only belief-system that took evil and suffering with absolute seriousness and, on Calvary, showed how it can be defeated: not removed or eradicated, but transformed and made an instrumental part of the purposes of an all-loving God.

Similarly, the Russian philosopher, Nicolas Berdyaev, has said of his own return to belief: 'My original religious impulse was bound up with a bitter feeling of discontent with and dissent from the world with its evil and corruption. And this was a first indication of my subsequent conviction that the existence of evil is not so much an obstacle to faith in God as a proof of God's existence, a challenge to turn towards that in which love triumphs over hatred, union over division and eternal life over death.'[4]

Without meaning and purpose not even the most satisfactory experiences can satisfy for long. With them, even the worst becomes at least tolerable because it is comprehensible, and this understanding is the beginning of wisdom. 'He who understands the Why can deal with almost any How', said Nietzsche.[5] Not that knowledge by itself heals: but because the seeming purposelessness of it all may well obscure for the sufferer the way to acceptance, growth and healing. The first question a patient asks when admitted to hospital is very often 'why should this happen to me?', 'why in this way?' It is part of the tragedy of the Book of Job that the sufferer is never given the answer as set out in the Prologue to the drama; he is merely silenced by the whirlwind and rebuked for asking the question! But it is the natural and necessary question that has to be faced if healing is to take place.

It is at the point when the existing belief-systems or set of values have broken down and fail to provide any satisfactory meaning or purpose that the possibility of other kinds can be entertained. Surely there must be a point in all this somewhere – there must be Something More? More satisfying, intelligible, compatible with human worth and dignity . . . In the film 'Educating Rita', a young Liverpool housewife finds herself unable wholeheartedly to join in the singing with her family in the pub. Her intoxication with new learning has turned the old culture to ashes in her mouth. She finds her mother next to her also silent and unable to join in. Together they ask: 'Surely there must be better songs than these?' Different, but not necessarily better, warns her tutor.

To adopt the Christian belief-system and way of life enables the believer to sing a different song. He finds his feet, says the Psalmist, 'in a large room', with walls, doors, windows, space to breathe and be. Distinct, but not necessarily separate from the many other rooms in the Father's house. Differently furnished (some would say that much of the furniture needs replacing and simplifying) and meeting different needs: but sharing common foundations and a common roof.

'System' is not perhaps the happiest word to use with reference to belief, even when used to denote a system of symbols and rituals. It implies a fixed, enclosed space, when the image should rather be one of movement and process than of a set of dogmas to be accepted or adopted en bloc. To live the cycle of the Christian Year is more like stepping onto an escalator, being carried by lift from floor to floor, than constructing a box, a house, even a 'laboratory of the Spirit'. True, St Paul speaks of the City whose architect is God. St Augustine, following Paul, uses this image so powerfully that his Two Cities became for centuries models for our thinking about the Church and the world. We warm to his homilies on the house whose foundations are faith, whose walls are hope and whose over-arching roof is charity.

And yet the City founded on the Rock, against which the gates of Hell will not prevail, is only one image of the Church. It has the disadvantage of setting one City over against another: drawing believers within the walls, pulling up the drawbridge, providing shelter for the faithful and protection from the world and the 'fiery darts of the Devil'. It implies that we know who is within and who outside the city walls, whereas the Gospel makes it clear that the 'God of Surprises' has a lot of time for those who think they are outside and little time for those who regard themselves as comfortably lodged within the shelter of the ramparts!

In 1827, before the 'Second Spring' of the Oxford Movement got under way, John Keble published his 'Christian Year'. Most of his poems/hymns have sunk into obscurity, for he was, as he would have been the first to admit, more of a preacher than a poet. He himself described his verses as mere 'crockery', and Geoffrey Faber calls him, despite his subsequent election to the chair of Poetry at Oxford, 'the Ella Wheeler Wilcox of his time.'[6] But it was an attempt to provide, in verse, a Baedeker guide through the liturgical landscape of the Church's year. More recently, Charles Williams gave us his 'New Christian Year', a rich and invaluable anthology with readings for each day, mainly from the great Classics of Spirituality, arranged for daily use. At a time when they were not widely known, he introduced many to the Desert Fathers, Meister Eckhart and William Law.

In what follows I do not attempt to duplicate, let alone replace, these admirable writers. I would invite the reader to step with me onto the escalator of the Christian Year: to move through the Seasons of the Spirit, enjoy the icons and explore the scenery. Some of the floors to be visited may contain little that grabs the attention or sets fire to the belly. Some may more profitably be revisited later. Almost the final entry in Williams' anthology (that for SS. Simon & Jude) is drawn from John Donne's sermons:

> In the Christian Church He hath given us means to be better today than yesterday and tomorrow than today. That grace which God offers us in the Church does not only fill that capacity which we have, but gives us a greater capacity than we had: and it is an abuse of God's grace not to improve it, or not to procure such further grace as that present grace makes us capable of.[7]

I am convinced that for every one who leaves or finds it impossible to join the community of faith through active unbelief, there must be a hundred who opt out from sheer boredom. It does not present them with the opportunity to grow and express their own unique individuality, make their own special contribution, sing their own song. And yet when the secular scene offers music of such jejune banality it may be time to explore another, different and perhaps better 'song'.

NOTES

1. Mary Douglas, 'Natural Symbols', London, 1970, p. 60.
2. Ibid., p. 73.
3. 'Faith in the City', the Report of the Archbishop of Canterbury's Commission on Urban Priority Areas, London, 1985. See especially ch. 9, 'Poverty, Employment and Work' which recalls William Temple's statement in the 1930s that 'unemployment is the most hideous of all social evils' (p. 207).
4. N. Berdyaev, 'Dream and Reality', London, 1950, p. 174.
5. I owe this reference to Donald Nicoll's 'The New Man', London 1981.
6. 'If one could imagine Keble deprived of his religious faith, he would have been a romantic and copious poet of the Lake School. Few, if any, of his critics would maintain that "The Christian Year" is good poetry. Fewer still, perhaps, would maintain that it is good religious poetry.' (G. Faber, 'Oxford Apostles', London, 1933, p. 91.) And that despite his subsequent election to the chair of poetry at Oxford!
7. 'The New Christian Year', Oxford, 1940, p. 280.

2

Winter into Spring

'Midwinter spring is its own season . . . '

There is no very good reason why we should begin our year with January 1st. The Jewish New Year, for example, is celebrated earlier, in the Autumn. Our ancestors would have started their year with Lady Day, the Feast of the Annunciation on March 25th, which has its own theological and agricultural rationale. Their intention, however, does not depart from the custom in Latin and English churches to make the Incarnation the pivotal point of the year. It is the season of Advent that marks the beginning of the Christian Year, and there could be no better time for new beginnings.

''Tis the yeare's midnight and it is the daye's', writes John Donne, celebrating what was traditionally (if wrongly) considered the shortest day in the year, St Lucy's Day, on December 13th.

The sunne is spent, and now his flasks
Send forth light squibs, no constant rayes;
The world's whole sap is sunk . . .
This houre her Vigill and her eve, since this
Both the yeare's and the daye's deep midnight is.

In a mood of deep depression, Donne feels the low point of the year reflected in his own low spirits. He feels like 'an ordinary nothing', unable to see the sun, his dead lover, or even to imagine its possible 'renewal'. Others in the Southern hemisphere, under the sign of the lustful Goat, may be enjoying their Summer. For him there is only Lucy's 'long night's festivall'.

The world into which Jesus was born knew its own 'year's midnight'. It is reflected most clearly in the deep cynicism of the 2nd/

3rd Century Preacher we know ironically enough as Ecclesiastes, the Mr Worldly-Wise-Man of the ancient world. For him all the natural joys, the many-splendoured attractions of a wonderful world, even ambition and the acquisition of new knowledge and fresh experience have all gone dead and dry as dust. There is nothing new under the sun. Although a later editor added a postscript and tried to make such a can of worms palatable to pious readers and more consistent with the philosophy of Wisdom literature, he cannot hide the Preacher's basic conclusion that all is vanity, human life has no meaning and all effort to improve it is futile. As Hobbes expressed it later in a famous epigram: 'No arts; no letters; no society; and which is worst of all, continual fear and danger of violent death; and the life of man, solitary, poor, nasty, brutish and short.'[1]

The year's midnight is a season experienced by the natural pessimist who, rejecting rose-tinted spectacles, takes a long, hard look at the human predicament and shudders at what he sees. 'I do not like the human race, I do not like its silly face . . . ' Sensitivity to suffering, human or animal, encourages scepticism; without the intervention of 'the gracious neighbour' or some 'happening' to surprise us, this may settle into fatalism, the bleakest cynicism and acute depression.

An actor who came late in his career to the great Greek Tragedies remarked that for the first time he appreciated the possibility of a world without forgiveness. In the Oresteia the inexorable treadmill of Fate rolls on, grinding the destiny of defenceless mortals under the heavy weight of Providence. There is no hope of redress, no possibility of escape for King Oedipus and his royal House; his life and the lives of all the others who are caught up in the tragedy contain none of the options that were presented to King Lear, Macbeth or Hedda Gabler. Lear, having made his choice, has to run his course, from tyranny to the ultimate destitution and the loss even of reason itself. But Shakespeare, writing in the Christian era (whatever his personal beliefs which we shall probably never know), leaves Lear at least the possibility of penitence as he holds the dead Cordelia in his arms. But he dies gently, among friends, reconciled to Kent, his loyal and dependable supporter . . .

THE ART OF WAITING

The season of Advent is concerned with ends and beginnings. Its prescribed liturgical readings seem to refer more to the Second or Final 'Coming' than to the First. For many this presents an immediate problem. It was generally expected that the appearance of Messiah would mark the beginning of the End: 'D' Day with the Normandy landings, perhaps, but not itself 'V' Day, the end of the War (or the world). Things would get bad: there would be wars persecutions, portents. But they should take courage, for the end, the time of liberation was at hand. It was a time for hope, not dread.

It seems that Jesus himself shared this assumption. At least he left his followers with the clear expectation that they had not long to wait for the end of all things to come upon them. Gradually they adjusted to the idea that there was to be no immediate 'Final Coming', and we can detect that adjustment taking place as the New Testament was being written. The urgency of 1 Thessalonians gives way to the steadier, long-term view of Ephesians, with its advice to the young Christian communities to order their lives in the way of peace and love.

Some saw in the cataclysmic event of Pentecost a kind of 'Coming' – for so it was, a coming in power, echoing Jesus' promise: 'I will not leave you desolate, I will come to you.' But they never lost sight of the ultimate truth that there would be an End, a fulfilment, an omega-point to which the whole process of creation and redemption was directed. Wisely, following his example, they refused to pin-point it with a specific date: it would be as foolish to put a label, 4004 AD, on the End as it was to put the label 4004 BC, on the Beginning.

Unfortunately, the subsequent history of the Church has shown no lack of those who disregard either his refusal to specify the day of his Coming or his injunction to 'watch'. The Montanists towards the end of the 2nd Century lived in daily expectation of a new visitation by the Holy Spirit. They were summoned to await the descent of the Heavenly Jerusalem at the chosen site of Pepuza in Asia Minor. They were but one of many apocalyptic groups which have sprung up whenever there has been danger of complacency and Christians have neglected to 'watch'. These Millenarians based their prophecies on a literal interpretation of Daniel 9 and Revelation 20, believing that the Final Coming would be preceded by 1000 years during which Christ would reign as King upon earth with the Saints before taking them with him into Heaven.

Such prophecies received a great boost in the Middle Ages with the approach of the magical year 1000 AD. Whether or not the approach of 2000 AD provokes a similar outburst, the passing of the expected moment has never dashed the hopes of enthusiastic 'watchers'. In our own day, Millenarianism has been a tenet of Irvingites, Mormons, Adventists and Jehovah's Witnesses. William Miller, founding prophet of the Adventists, confidently predicted 1843 as the date of the Coming: he subsequently revised the date to the following year, but when that passed he retired from the scene, acknowledging his mistake. The movement was carried on by Ellen White, an epileptic visionary, who in the course of her 83 years of life gave several dates on which she said the world was to end. Contemporary Adventists are more cautious and believe we are 'nearing the end of a probationary time which will only close with the completion of the Church's work.' The founder of the Jehovah's Witnesses, Pastor Charles Russell, calculated that the Second Advent had occurred, invisibly, in 1874: he subsequently revised his dates several times. Judge Rutherford who followed was more circumspect. He taught that Christ had returned invisibly in 1914 to usher in the new era, after which Armageddon would be fought, Jehovah would prevail and the elect 144,000 would be gathered into his Kingdom.

'ARMAGEDDON'

Such vagaries on the lunatic fringes of enthusiasm might be dismissed as illustrations of the infinite capacity of the human spirit to believe anything, however preposterous, provided it covers our nagging anxieties with some mantle of security. But the emergence of the Moral Majority in the U.S.A, led by Jerry Falwell and renamed the Liberty Foundation, with its growing political influence, casts a more sinister shadow over our lives. They see the political spectrum in dualistic terms; their firm conviction that the 'Communist Menace' is Antichrist and that Armageddon may well be encountered in nuclear war reinforces for them the inevitability of confrontation and nuclear holocaust. 'It will be God's instrument for the punishment of sinners and the destruction of evil. Believers – whether the Israel Army or born-again Christians – will be saved miraculously.'[2]

The fact that such views, it is claimed, are shared by over 10 million Americans and received some sympathetic support from President Reagan and his Secretary of Defence makes it the more incumbent on mainstream believers to develop a balanced and critical approach to the teaching of the Second Coming, Apocalyptic and 'Armageddon Theology'. Any glib equation of the Beast, Babylon or Antichrist with 'godless Russia', 'American cowboy imperialism' or even the Church of Rome only feeds Cold War attitudes, deepens anxiety and makes detente and peace-building more difficult. A reading of the Book of Revelation, in fact, should remind us of God's continual judgment on all human institutions: the State in the New Testament is not just God's instrument for justice in the world – it is also the Beast. It should give us a vision of the New Heaven and the New Earth: not fatalistic dread of the future, but the sure knowledge that (in Dame Julian's words) 'all things shall be well and all manner of thing shall be well.' That is true Christian hope, grounded in Scripture and the promises of Christ, sending us back into the demanding, frustrating present, with all its ambivalences and complexities.

However clearly this provides the backdrop, it need not distract us from the action of the play itself. The word used for 'Final Coming', Parousia, has a double meaning; it also denotes 'Presence' and points us to the deeper and more urgent truth that Christ is always coming, just when we least expect him, like a burglar (says Paul) in the night. He catches us off our guard, looking the other way –

> for Christ plays in ten thousand places,
> Lovely in limbs, and lovely in eyes not his
> To the Father through the features of men's faces

– and we miss him. Time Past, the historical record of the first coming, and Time Future, the promise of the Final Coming, are both contained in Time Present, the Now when we encounter the Christ in love and friendship, but also in fear and trembling. How we meet him – in the weak and vulnerable neighbour, in prayer and sacrament, in all encounters with reality, will determine all the other meetings, including the final meeting, face to face. Just as the way we meet our physical death will largely be determined, for good or ill, by the way we deal with the little deaths along the way, experience of loss, separation, disappointment, bereavement, the hanging-on and letting-go.

EARLY WARNINGS

But Advent is just as much about beginnings as it is about ends. At the gate of the Christian Year stands a strange, nebulous figure from the 7th Century BC, the prophet Habakkuk, a contemporary of the more familiar Jeremiah.[3] In a series of vivid images he sees the Babylonian army, the oppressive invader, inexorably advancing on the tiny Jewish people. He describes their fearsome weaponry, the speed and violence of their war-machine. 'Where are you, Lord?' he asks, 'what are you *doing*?' Like Job and the Psalmists he dares question the ways of Providence: how long, O Lord, how long . . .?

So he climbs a tower, to seek solitude and to watch for signs of the invading army. Like the Psalmist, he waits patiently on God – waits, watches and listens. The answer, when it comes, is couched in the maddening obscurity of all oracular utterances:

> For the vision is yet for an appointed time, but at the end it shall speak and not lie: though it tarry, wait for it; because it will surely come, it will not tarry. (2.3)

That – and very little else for his encouragement. The saying that 'the just shall live by faith', which formed the key-stone of Paul's theology and the great slogan of the Reformation, probably meant 'those who endure to the end will be saved', 'those who are loyal to God will survive the hard rain a'falling.' There are some fierce denunciations of domestic vices in true prophetic vein, a prayer 'in wrath remember mercy', and we hear no more. But Habukkuk has climbed his tower, looked for the dawn and found his perspective corrected. And the believer who waits with alert expectancy on God climbs his own tower with the prophet and makes his prayer his own: 'Like as the watchman looks for the morning, so do our eyes look to you, O Lord; come with the dawning of the day and make yourself known to us in the breaking of bread. For you are our God, for ever and ever.'

The other prophet who stands at the gate of the Christian Year is the one known to the Orthodox as Prodromos, the Forerunner, and to most of us as John the Baptist; at the door of the year, as the font stands at the door into the church building. Before we embark on the year we are invited to withdraw: reculer pour mieux sauter. The place/period/posture of withdrawal is described as Desert. The pattern is that of Jesus himself who used the space to prepare for his life's work. What we know as the Mount of Temptation may well represent years of quiet preparation, withdrawal and contemplation; some of the time spent, possibly, with contemporary communities like the Essenes, learning from a guru or 'staretz' like the Prophet of Righteousness of the Dead Sea Scrolls. Of these 'hidden years' we are given the one glimpse, that deep and intense conflict with the powers of evil. Yet the period of withdrawal provided the key, the launching-pad for the three intensive years that followed.

We find the same pattern in the life of St Paul who, in the earliest account we have of his personal history (Gal. 1, 17–18), describes his withdrawal to 'Arabia', presumably Transjordan, in the region between Damascus and the Red Sea. He himself wishes to emphasise that during this retreat period (given as three years but probably one full year and parts of two others), he developed his thought independently of the Church of Jerusalem. He had received his own commission as Apostle to the Gentiles and needed space to prepare for it. The headlong narrative of Acts gives little conception of this long process of silent preparation: just as the urgency of the Gospel narratives virtually ignores the hidden years of Jesus' own training and development.

DESERT

The Desert provides space to look around, 'consider the heavens the work of thy hands, the moon and the stars which thou hast ordained', not hemmed in by clutter, locked in a perpetual traffic-jam. There is time to be, without the frenzy of activity imposed by guilt or social conscience. It simplifies the complexities and half-tones that obscure decision, down to the bare, dry bones of Ezekiel's vision. We are enabled to correct the biased perspective and silence the internal atmospherics that baffle the listening ear. 'Our religion begins with the word in the desert,' says John Drury, 'the death outside the city. It is the function of the prophet to remind us of that, in season and out.' But it remains the most difficult as it is the most indispensable task of any contemporary spirituality to create a desert, a stillness, at the heart of the city.

When Charles de Foucauld[4] established his hermitage in the Sahara, he built a wall around it no higher than two feet, to allow travellers, visitors from neighbouring oases, to climb over when they wanted to talk. He had created a space; what he did in his way, with dry stone, we have to do, each in a different way. Russians speak of the 'poustinia': a kind of hermitage or peace-centre, a space to withdraw and be, but even more, to be renewed. You can create 'poustinia' in your home or garden or within your own heart. But its walls can never be high enough to exclude your neighbours and prevent them being invited, on occasion, to enter and share the peace.

Out of the silence of the desert comes the voice: 'Make straight a highway for our God.' Not a comforting demand; it requires us to deal with the crookednesses, inconsistencies, evasions and half-truths: the twists of illusion and self-deception that obscure those truths we are too frightened to hear. The timid and the time-servers rush in to emphasise the relativity, even irrelevance of a truth that is rarely valid for all time, only in the present moment, for us and our salvation. They prefer the darkness of illusion to the light of the Truth that might set them free. The task of the prophet is to make us think the unthinkable, digest the unpalatable. It is one from which the best, even an Amos, have shrunk: the truer they speak, the more likely they are to be stoned. And they speak most convincingly when they admit they may even be wrong. 'I beseech you in the bowels of Christ,' said Cromwell to the General Assembly of the Church of Scotland, 'think it possible you may be mistaken.'

There has never been any shortage of false prophets: the old dope-pedlar with his powdered happiness, 'all the easy speeches that comfort cruel men', the slick persuaders with painless solutions to complex problems. Only trust to North Sea Oil and the balance of payments, nuclear energy and advanced technology and all shall be well. That, says the prophet of doom and destruction, is a mere extension of Victorian self-confidence, belief in the power of education and the need for Samuel Smiles' self-improvement. None of these benefits, however desirable in themselves, will necessarily make you any happier, more loving, at peace with yourself and your neighbour. And your whole structure may collapse tomorrow like a pack of cards under the impending cataclysm, world famine or nuclear war.

The important thing, says the prophet of the Good Life, is to simplify: return to the natural rhythms, organic farming, profit-sharing and the balanced life. The Kingdom is within . . . Be reasonable, says the prophet of Moderation; don't run to extremes – in our age 'the road to holiness passes through the world of action' . . .

This fear of 'polarising' particularly afflicts English/Anglican believers who adhere historically to the 'Via Media'. At its worst it is a stance which attempts to embrace the widest spectrum of truth within the embrace of a 'Broad Church Movement': an uncomfortable position caricatured as sitting on the fence with both ears to the ground! At its best it combines belief and action, the imminent and the transcendent, giving full value to each. It might be seen as a true blending of traditions represented par excellence by the Orthodox and the Society of Friends. It is represented symbolically by the Cross which holds together the vertical and the horizontal dimensions: a historical, incarnational faith, firmly rooted in tradition, with an openness to the action of the Spirit for the liberation of humankind.

To pursue moderation in all things may well lead to embracing everything by turns and nothing long. The true 'Middle Way' lies not in the mean between the two extremes, but in holding both extremes together. It is not the watering down of truth and dilution of doctrines to suit our convenience. That would lead to a vapid indifferentism where anything goes and anyone's opinion, however ill-informed, is as good as anyone else's. To get the balance and perspective right is perhaps the most demanding task in contemporary religious and political thinking.

'It hath been the wisdom of the Church of England,' states the Preface to the Prayer Book with delightful immodesty about its liturgy, 'to keep the mean between the two extremes, of too much stiffness in refusing, and of too much easiness in admitting any variation from it.' If we apply this to doctrine or ideology we appreciate the problem: how do we pursue equality, even at its lowest level in equality of opportunity, without setting intolerable limits to basic human freedoms? How do we 'set the people free' and not leave them defenceless against the skilful manipulators of public opinion and the pedlars of esoteric ideologies masquerading as ultimate truth? Finding the right balance between freedom and authority has been an ideal seldom achieved in Church or State.

Leaders of New Nations with their emerging ideologies have to find their own 'balance'. Our students in the University of Zambia had the greatest difficulty in relating Western European culture and technology to their own. Some embraced it so wholeheartedly that they found themselves profoundly alienated from the beliefs and values of their (mostly rural) family backgrounds. Others equally passionately rejected it as a damaging import, the expression of colonial exploitation and oppression from which political independence had set them free. To accept the insights and benefits of Western culture and blend them with all that is best in traditional African culture was and remains an almost superhuman demand. Today it faces the indigenous churches as insistently as it faces the political parties and liberation movements of the Third World.

AGAINST THE STREAM

Though we only hear it in the clipped tones of a Manifesto, the message of John the Baptist is addressed to the church and society of his day. He is depicted as one who refuses to follow fashion (no 'reed bowing before the wind') or party-line, but pursues truth wherever it leads and whatever it costs. He is non-attached to the ambitions of the upwardly mobile and their obsession with success (no 'man dressed in posh clothes'): critical, to the point of nonconformity, of the religious Establishment. A prophet in the sense that he is a loner, one who swims against the stream, pursues and demands integrity above all else. He stands up to be counted and pays the inevitable penalty.

John quotes Malachi, resembles Elijah and appears almost out of nowhere, from the desert. He stands firmly in the prophetic tradition that stretches from Socrates to Gandhi, from Amos and Jeremiah to Bonhoeffer and Archbishop Romero, in his refusal to compromise with any religious or political Establishment. We are not told what the religious authorities thought of him, only what he unquestionably thought of them. Like Jesus, however, he was accepted as a Teacher and addressed as Rabbi (Luke 3, 13).[5] His replies to questions from Whitehall and the City were, in contrast to his fierce denunciation of the Church, surprisingly liberal and tolerant. True, if the revenue-officers, who depended very largely on a form of licensed extortion, had followed his advice they would soon have lost their livelihood. But they are not denounced as collaborators or social outcasts – they are simply reminded of their duty to be fair. They are told to resist the particular temptations of their profession; as are the members of the security forces for whom strong-arm tactics, bullying and blackmail, would have been an accepted feature of colonial rule.

There can be no feature of our world that speaks so tragically of its loss of civilised values as the increasingly accepted practice of torture. The infliction of intolerable pain on often innocent suspects (even on children) by ever more ingenious and diabolical means is nothing short of barbarous. Moreover, no security forces or special branch anywhere in the world can be totally exonerated. It is a fair measure of the stature of John that he selected for particular comment the three features in his own society which he might most strongly criticise in ours. The need for fair shares between the privileged and under-privileged, over-employed and under-employed: economic justice and a fair wage, a just profit, without exorbitant returns and capital gains: the exercise of authority without resort to undue force and the meeting of force with counter-force, violence with greater violence. Three areas where our own society is most vulnerable to criticism.

This was the overture to the New Age, the glimmer of light before the promised dawn and the first scene in the divine drama of redemption. But the overture is announced not with a gentle dawn chorus so much as a clap of thunder. The significance of John's water-baptism lay in its cleansing, healing symbolism: it was a sign of forgiveness extended now not merely to Gentiles being initiated into Judaism but universally, even to those who confidently claim 'Abraham as our father' (Luke 3, 8). Like many another revivalist preacher, he proclaims the imminence of divine judgment and the promise of forgiveness. And this begins at the centre, at the very heart of Jewish faith, with the Temple itself. The Fourth Gospel may well be historically as well as theologically right in placing the Cleansing of the Temple at the opening, not the closing stages of Jesus' ministry.

Moreover, the sequel tells of a leading ecclesiastic, Nicodemus, being confronted by the demand for a fresh start – new birth and the gift of the Spirit. Baffling, no doubt, for the night visitor who is depicted as an honest and genuine enquirer (John 3, 2): but for us, the readers, a natural development of the process that began with the Baptist's summons to repentance; took on, at Cana, symbolic shape in the replacing of water-cleansing by the transforming power of the Gospel; then found its climax in a public and highly political act, a direct and provocative attack on institutional religion itself. It is because Jesus, as a pious Jew, makes his criticism from within, not outside the institution that his act of creative disobedience is so effective. He speaks as a true son of Israel: the Psalmist quoted ('zeal for your house will devour me' – Psalm 69, 9) has just said:

> I have become a stranger to my brothers:
>   an alien to my mother's sons

and the power and the passion with which he is impelled to act spring from the depths of that alienation. It is to his own people that he has come.

BACK TO BASICS

The Christian Year opens where the Gospel begins, with judgment at the heart of the institutional Church. It may 'speak what it knows', but the yawning credibility gap between its pretensions and its performance, the truth proclaimed and the truth 'done', makes it hard for the world to hear what is being said. When

Gandhi marched to the sea or Martin Luther King marched on Washington the act and the word were one. When we make fine speeches on the evils of Apartheid but, by virtue of our vast investments in South African firms, connive at our continued profits from it, we cannot escape the charge that 'these people make fine noises with their lips, but their hearts are far from me.' Advent, through the mouth of the prophets, demands that we look to our integrity: make straight the petty dishonesties and clever pieces of double-think: and deal with the racism, greed, sexism and militarism that lie as deeply embedded in our own society as was commercial exploitation in the Temple.

One of the ways we find we are 'straightened' is by constant reference to Scripture. Advent points us to the Bible as the Baptist points us to the Christ. Not to find knock-down arguments and answers to besetting problems; but in the sense that we look to Magna Charta as guaranteeing our constitutional freedoms, or to the Hippocratic Oath as the founding charter of medical professional practice. If we regard the Scriptures, in the words of the English Coronation Service, as the 'lively oracles of God' they are 'oracular' not as the Sybil or Old Moore's Almanac might be said to be oracular, but in the OED sense, as a reliable 'guide, test or indicator; authoritative, profoundly wise or mysterious adviser, judge, prophet.'

When we turn to the Jewish Scriptures we are presented with three inescapable questions:

(1) 'What does the Lord require of you?' (Micah's question – 6, 8). We do not find any treatise or dissertation on justice, mercy or humility: not even advice on how such desirable virtues may be cultivated. They are seen as a sine qua non, a requirement; what life and religion are all about, what it means to be human. We may argue how they can be applied, for instance, to industrial disputes or the practice of abortion; what we cannot escape in the Judaeo-Christian tradition is this three-fold requirement of justice, mercy and humility before God.

(2) 'Why do you hide your face?' (Job's question – 13, 24); a variant of the question: 'Why do the wicked flourish and the innocent suffer?' Why does God move in a mysterious way his wonders to perform? It is the question that rises like the smoke from the chimneys of Auschwitz and has dominated the history of

the Jewish people down the ages. Job's agony is not simply brought on by the pain, grief and deprivation he feels; he can endure the boils and the dung-heap, even the high-minded moralising of his friends and the despair of his wife. What he finds unendurable is not knowing why it has all happened. In persisting with his question he retains the last shreds of his humanity. He may seem to have lost everything, but he has not lost his integrity.

(3) 'What is "Man" that you should care for him?' (The Psalmist's question – 8, 4). More basic even than 'what?' or 'why?' is the question 'what for?', the demand for purpose as well as meaning. Job is told that he has no right to ask that question, any more than the pot has to ask why it is made in this particular shape and no other. The Preacher, as we have seen, finds no meaning or purpose anywhere, at least in this life. The world is a cosmic yawn. But Jews are a very argumentative people; they have never ceased to ask God questions, to bargain with him, like Abraham, and even, like Noah in Andre Obey's delightful play, to answer him back. The Bible, in its maddening, many-hued variety, carries on the argument like a cosmic conversation. 'Search the Scriptures,' says John, 'for they contain Eternal Life' – all that you really need; not the answers to all your questions but the right questions to ask.

WAITING & WORKING

It may now be apparent why Advent is the only conceivable season to begin the Christian Year. It is essentially the time of waiting, yearning in hope and expectation. The whole creation, the victim of frustration, unable to realise its true potential, 'waits with eager expectation' (Rom. 8, 19) for an end to futility and meaninglessness. 'The world in solemn stillness lay . . . ' The image is one of child-birth; we 'groan inwardly', waiting for the waters to break in the moment of release and new birth. Fully to share this mood of waiting you need to be black, female or, in some seemingly inevitable way, disadvantaged. That is why Jesus called the 'poor' the true inheritors of the Kingdom – whether it be the materially poor or 'the poor in spirit', those who know their true status is one of absolute dependence on God's generosity. Only when you are truly aware of your creaturehood, confronted by the unfathomable depth of your need, can you appreciate what you are being liberated *from* or *for*:

> to see the stars
> through prison-bars
>
> is to see them with
> new eyes, as if for the first time.

Only the family on the bread-line knows the true value of a £5 note; only the prisoner or hostage, held on an indeterminate sentence, knows what it means to 'hope against hope'. A father may experience, through empathy, the pangs of child-birth; but only the mother who has known the long Advent months of waiting can receive the unutterable joy of release that is Christmas:

> Heaviness may endure for a night,
> but joy cometh in the morning.

Some have misunderstood 'waiting' as a posture of passivity, fatalistic resignation, 'waiting for Godot'. As if the prisoner simply ticked off the days on the calendar, waiting for the train that never seems to arrive. On the contrary, waiting on God and working for God belong together and are not separable or inconsistent. Those who have been prisoners of war tell us it was only by contriving continual means of escape that they survived. It was not enough simply to hope for the day of release – their very humanity depended on their actively working to advance it. Survivors of concentration camps remember the ones who stopped working; they very soon smoked their last cigarettes, curled up and died. Pregnancy is no passive state, but one that encourages intense concentration, alertness to every signal and movement, a blend of waiting and working.

In our own time, however, we are less likely to be seduced by passivity and to fall victims of navel-gazing Quietism: the siren voice is that of activism, which is working without waiting. Rather than be accused of being collaborators, settling for the status quo, we are tempted to rush into the arms of any resistance movement that promises an end to alienation and despair. Our culture demands instant response and satisfaction; it derides patience as mere plodding; in its demand for total revolution it dismisses the piecemeal reformer as that most despised creature, the white bourgeois liberal, 'the SDP at prayer'. Of all the delicate balances to be kept, that between action and contemplation, between the flurry of feverish activity and the paralysis of seeing no point in any action whatever, is the hardest to maintain. Narrow is the way between this Scylla and Charybdis and few there be that find it.

OPENCAST CHRISTMAS

The advantage of making Advent the launching-pad for the coming year is that it puts Christmas, the Feast of Incarnation, back where it belongs – as the basis for Exodus Theology and the drama of Redemption. The crib is rescued from mythological romanticism and points the way to Cross and Resurrection. The Madonna's birth-pangs are seen in the context of the cosmic labour to bring forth a new era. There is always a tendency to privatise and domesticate the Birth of Jesus, as we do his Death (speaking of 'My Cross', 'Their Calvary' etc.); that is our way of dealing with the passage of time and the differences of culture. Birmingham seems as remote from Bethlehem as Das Kapital from the Book of Revelation.

Mediaeval carols spoke differently, of Alpha and Omega, the beginning and the end; the best of them had a pervading sense of contrast between the Now and the Not Yet. The English tend to quarry much of their theology not from books and commentaries, but from 'opencast' hymns and liturgy, The carols which have worn best, all too narrowly limited in popular consciousness to Christmas, have retained much of its meaning and magic and made the deepest mysteries both wonderful and homely. Everyone knows that St Francis of Assisi invented the crib; it is not so widely known that it was Franciscans who gave us carols. Remembering how their founder had told them to be God's Troubadours, 'jongleurs de Dieu', they claimed the pop songs of their day and danced them into the liturgy.

> Tomorrow shall be my dancing day;
> I would my true love so did chance

Remembering how their founder had told them to be God's Troubadours, 'jongleurs de Dieu', the Franciscans claimed the pop songs of their day and danced them into the liturgy.

To see the legend of my play
To call my true love to my dance.
  Sing O my love, O my love, my love,
  This have I done for my true love.

In a manger laid and wrapped I was
So very poor, this was my chance,
Between an ox and a silly ass
To call my true love to my dance . . .

The word 'carol' is defined by the OED as originally 'a ring-dance with a song', derived from the Greek 'choraules', a flute-player for chorus-dancing. Chaucer can write in his 14th Century Romaunt of the Rose:

'Come, and if it lyké you
To dauncen dauncith with us now.'
And I withouté tarrying,
Wente into the karolying.[6]

No doubt, St Francis would have gone in with him more readily than into a formal 'Festival of Nine Lessons and Carols' – but there is room for both!

God's troubadours do not only give us permission to celebrate – they command it: 'Buvez bien, buvez bien . . . ' But with the merriment they retain the mystery of 'Heilige Nacht, Stille Nacht.'

He came all so still,
Like the dew in Aprille . . .

The Christ-Child lay on Mary's heart
  His hair was like a fire.
(O weary, weary is the world
  But here the world's desire.)

The magic is irresistible; and yet the real world keeps breaking in. Herod the King and his raging; the holly and its berry red as any blood, its prickle as sharp as any thorn and its bark as bitter as any gall – they serve to remind us of what is to come later. If the Child sleeps now it is because there will be little sleep later for the nights spent in prayer on the hills of Galilee. In the best carols the beginning reminds us of the end, the First Coming of the Second. The homeless stranger 'cradled in a manger, for us facing every danger', brings today's homeless, the thousands sleeping on the streets of our cities or on the Ethiopian hills, crowding into our midst.

There is a universalism in the best carols which rescues us from the privatised, domesticated Christ. It is triumphantly proclaimed by the 4th Century hymn of Prudentius:

> He is Alpha; from that fountain
> All that is and hath been flows;
> He is Omega, of all things
> Yet to come the mystic close
> Evermore and evermore . . .

It is echoed in Sidney Carter's

> Every star shall sing a carol: every creature high and low,
> Come and praise the King of Heaven, by whatever name you know.

And it finds expression in Alice Meynell's fine poem 'Christ in the Universe', which ends

> O be prepared, my soul!
> To read the inconceivable, to scan
> The myriad forms of God those stars unroll
> When, in our turn, we show to them a Man.[7]

The Child transcends all time and all culture-barriers; he is 'the weary world's desire.' However daring, even presumptuous, such an assertion it is implicit at the heart of the Gospels, in the presence of the Magi, kneeling before the 'Light that lightens everyone who comes into this world.'

'WHEN THE SHORT DAY IS BRIGHTEST . . . '

What is implicit in Christmas becomes explicit in Epiphany.

Known to the Orthodox as 'the Feast of Lights' it proclaims the Light to lighten the Gentiles, for all time and every culture. As the original Christmas it was only displaced by the Emperor Constantine for pragmatic reasons: it was convenient to celebrate the Son's Birthday on the traditional day of honour for Sol Invictus, the Unconquered Sun. The Armenian and lesser Orthodox Churches still keep January 6th as their Christmas and regard December 25th as a nouveau riche Johnny-come-lately. We who have seen our Festival largely taken over by the Saturnalia may secretly envy them for their single-minded adherence to ancient custom!

Between the new Christmas and the old we welcome the inauguration of the secular New Year. As the Feast of Circumcision it has not, for obvious reasons, stirred English hearts as Hogmanay, overshadowing Christmas, has for the Scots. As until the middle of the 18th Century the year was thought to begin with Lady Day, on March 25th, January 1st has never acquired much religious significance. The ASB records it principally as 'The Naming of Jesus'. This is certainly preferable to John Keble's idea that

> The year begins with Thee
> And thou beginn'st with woe,
> To let the world of sinners see
> That blood for sin must flow.

Some still welcome the dark stranger bearing bread, coal and salt, the symbols of life, warmth and hospitality. Dark, because mysterious and representing the unknown events of the coming year. But apart from the bells ringing out the old, ringing in the new, January 1st has reverted to what it originally was, the Kalends on which the riotous festival of Saturnalia was observed in ancient Rome. To compete with this, John Wesley's attempt to concentrate our minds on the sober and serious themes of a Watch Night Service has never stood much of a chance.

The swift passage from Christmas to Epiphany embraces the transition of the Gospel from the local, particular and historical event (Jesus born in Palestine) to the general and universal truth (Jesus Salvator Mundi, the same yesterday, today and for ever). If it is true that the two earliest slogans current in the early Church were 'Iesous Christos' (Messiah) and 'Kyrios Iesous' (Jesus is Lord), they mark, in shorthand form, the movement of thought that can be traced in the Gospels themselves. Indeed, though this may be presumptuous, it may even be traced back to the developing consciousness of Jesus himself. Whereas initially he seems to have confined his work to 'the lost sheep of the house of Israel' – 'he came to his own' – in the later stages the scope was widened to include the Gentiles and 'the world'. What we see as development in his own thinking may, of course, be the development of the early Christian movement through which our Gospels have been filtered. We know that the tension between the Judaizers and the Gentile converts nearly split the Church in a conflict that was only resolved by the passionate pleas and skilful diplomacy of St Paul. If he had lost this crucial battle, the Church of Jerusalem and those who insisted that converts had to be fully obedient to Jewish Law might have gone the way of the Old Believers in Russia, to the ghetto.

'NEVER & ALWAYS'

The tension between the particular and the universal is resolved for the Orthodox in their celebration of Epiphany as the Baptism of Christ. He was baptised, Christed, 'to do all that righteousness demands'; it was his way of announcing the fulfilment of his people's expectations. He was marked out as God's special Person: 'This is my Son, the Beloved; hear him.' All baptism, ours or his, involves choice; we choose to say 'yes' in response to the divine invitation to 'enter the Kingdom.' This Way, often referred to as 'the scandal of particularity', does not rule out other 'ways in' and different responses to the invitation: only that this is the way for me, for us. Ultimately (though for them the path home may open up a vastly different landscape, unfamiliar to many of us) for all humanity. This truth is presented in the Epiphany, the unveiling of the mystery of Love to the Gentiles.

Hence we do not deny, what the earliest Christians affirmed, that 'there is no salvation in anyone else at all, for there is no other name under heaven granted to men, by which we may receive salvation.' What must be resisted very strongly is making that name, Love, God's 'Word', coterminous with the Church or even with Christian religion. That would be to take the way of the early Judaizers of the Jerusalem Church – to reduce the Name to a rule-book, a new Law. Jesus is not the property of the Church; nor is 'Christianity', insofar as we can speak of that at all, the only true path to salvation. To reduce faith to 'religion' is equivalent to reducing Love to Law. And that, in spite of intense pressures, the Church has always successfully resisted. I believe we can say no less than Bishop Lesslie Newbiggin:

> To claim finality for Jesus Christ is not to assert that the majority of men will some day be Christians or to assert that all others will be damned. It is to claim that commitment to him is the way in whch men can become truly aligned to the ultimate end for which all things were made.[8]

Such a claim would not be abhorrent to a Gandhi or a Simone Weil, neither of whom submitted to baptism, but each of whom received a particular, personal Epiphany. Their route may not be ours, nor ours theirs: but their wisdom and undoubted holiness has enriched us all. They and their like serve to remind us of the continuing tension between the Now and the Not Yet, Church and Kingdom, religion and faith, the historical particular and the universal truth.

It has become almost a cli to see our task as not to bring Christ where he is not, but to find him where he has already preceded us, within the forms and experience of those who do not yet recognise him. To 'read their Scriptures in the light of Christ'; 'relate their apprehension of divinity to the object of Christian hope'; 'put away 'confessional pride and all the feelings of cultural or historical superiority' and follow 'the Christ-like way of self-fulfilment through the other.' The supreme task, says an Arab Orthodox writer, Metropolitan Georges Khodr, 'is to identify all the Christic values in other religions, to show them Christ as the bond which unites them and his love as their fulfilment.'[9]

Certainly, there is an intolerable arrogance in claiming that 'we' have the whole truth: Orthodoxy is my doxy, Heterodoxy is everyone else's. There is also a false tolerance in pretending that 'we're all going the same way really' (indifferentism); or 'we're all climbing the same mountain by different routes' (syncretism). To believe that 'Christ is the light that lightens everyone who comes into this world' places the believer under obedience to the Spirit who will guide us, step by step, into all Truth. To that obedience and exploration we invite our neighbours: to travel with us and make their own discoveries to enrich us all. 'Woe is me if I do not proclaim the Gospel,' we cry with St Paul, however weak my grasp of it and however pathetic my attempt to live it (do the truth). But the privilege of proclaiming never overrides the prior responsibility to listen; because the courage of our convictions also involves the courage to stand alongside the other and even to find, with Blake, that

> The Vision of Christ that thou dost see
> Is my vision's greatest enemy.

The Babel of religious propaganda emanating from Belfast, Teheran or the Bible Belt does not encourage us to think we listen any more attentively today than in the days of Savonarola and the Inquisition. Nevertheless, it is true of the religious as of the political dialogue that 'we must love one another or die.'

As the Taizé community has reminded us, you have never really listened to your neighbour until you have come to the very point of agreeing he is right. Only when you have said your fullest 'Yes' can you then go on to say 'Yes But . . .' Listening attentively is at the heart of the praying and witnessing life of the believer: giving God and your neighbour your undivided attention. But with the persistent, nagging divisions between us how is this possible? Mission and unity belong together, feeding and frustrating each other; so it is to prayer for Christian Unity that we are invited in the season of Epiphany.

WINDOWS OF OPPORTUNITY

'Division is not just clearly contrary to Christ's will. It is a scandal to the world and a hindrance to the sacred task of preaching the Gospel to every creature' (Vatican 2). We who are entrusted with the Gospel of reconciliation are unable to be reconciled with one another. 'See how these Christians love each other,' their neighbours once observed – and yet are unable to live with each other! There is no feud so bitter or so hard to resolve as a family feud: no war as bloody as a civil war. While this can flare up into open conflict in Belfast or Beirut, it simmers silently in families where the members cannot break bread together across the denominational barriers. We each of us have folk-memories and unfinished business with the past to be dealt with.

We should not, however, underestimate the real advances that have been made. In the present Century, since the Ecumenical Movement was born at Edinburgh in 1910, communities that had grown apart for 400 years have begun to grow together. There is today a new spirit of openness and tolerance: deep friendships have replaced the old rivalries and competitiveness. We have discovered Judaism and perceived the Holy Spirit at work in the Eastern religions, and the discovery has changed us. Many of the old dogmas and certainties seem now blinkered and arrogant. Certainly we have lost power and influence and with that some of the trappings of privilege –

> God bless the squire and his relations
> And keep us in our proper stations!

But this enables the Cross to be seen as a sign of judgment and victory, not as an instrument of oppression and manipulation. We have renewed our liturgy and common life; Catholics have discovered the Bible and Protestants the Eucharist. In a Century that has seen the change from the horse-drawn bus to Concorde and inter-planetary travel Christendom has not stood still.

Nor should we underestimate the real costs in coming together. We are divided not merely by prejudice but by principles, deeply felt and strongly maintained. It is hardly likely that differences, for instance, over the necessity for believers' baptism; authority and the place of laity in decision-making; the sacramental principle and Papal Infallibility – will be resolved in our lifetime. But what is required of us is not to commit intellectual suicide and betray the truth as we see it. We do not seek uniformity – that has never existed in the Church since its first beginnings – but rather a pluriformity which is reflected in our own increasingly pluralistic society (see below).

POLYGLOT . . .

Over the past half century we have experienced a convergence of cultures which had previously been geographically separated and colonially subjugated. Our own polyglot culture has absorbed the great pre-war wave of Jewish immigrants with their infusion of European and predominantly Jewish cultural life: the American influx during World War 2, the immigration of families from Asia and the Third World after the War – these have all served to widen our cultural vision far beyond the confines of Western Europe. Millions have travelled farther and faster than ever before and returned to view their own culture with different eyes.

Socially, we are no longer victims of Jingoistic attitudes to the superiority of Anglo-Saxon ways. Cecil Rhodes' dream of painting the map red, covering the world with 'British Civilization' survives only in the wilder flights of the Powellian imagination. In fact, our hegemony is seen to depend largely on technological skills, climatic good fortune, the cross-fertilization of different cultural influences (Greek, Roman, Celtic, Hebrew), or just on brute force –

> Whatever happens we have got
> The maxim gun and they have not.

Our self-confidence, in short, is so badly shaken that many of the young reject 'Western' values as barren or positively harmful in their materialism and aggressiveness and turn to the East for enlightenment and inspiration. Nor is it just the 'alternative' fringe that is affected. The Blues, Reggae, Rock, Folk and Protest songs have transformed popular culture; our eating and drinking habits have significantly changed since the War; whereas Indian and Chinese food was once a rare middle-class adventure, today every town boasts its Taj Mahal beside its Wimpy Bar.

. . . AND PLURIFORM

All these changes have immeasurably enriched our social and cultural scene. But the religious scene has been no less affected. The Euro-centred view of our faith is as outdated as a pre-Copernican view of the Universe: Jung, Toynbee and the sociologists of religion have prepared us for the revolution, but the effect on bible-based orthodoxy in our day has been as severe as the Darwinian revolution a century ago. This is particularly marked in the spheres of religious education and Christian mission or missiology. Whereas even in 1944, with the Butler Act, our school system and those for whom it catered were considered sufficiently homogeneous for Christian teaching and worship to be imposed (or at least imparted) throughout the country; today this is seen as increasingly anomalous and even oppressive indoctrination. The cry of 'European cultural tribalism' from secularists and even from Christians has led to a demand for a more open-ended syllabus and greater attention to the insights afforded by other religious traditions.

The Ecumenical Movement today, while continuing to search for a unity that will preserve the identity and special characteristics of the bodies that compose it, is not afraid to take a lead in inter-faith dialogue. What does it mean to be living in different rooms (John 14, 2) under the one roof of the Father's house? To live, not just as a family with all the trials and tensions of family life, but as a family of families, with a common focus, the character and spirit of Christ?

Stephen Sykes has warned us that we have to be pluriform not only in function (Rom. 12, 6; 1 Cor. 12), but also in belief; partly because of the varying life-experience in which that belief is moulded, partly because we lack 'an unambiguous focal point of absolute authority'. In all this we may be nearer to the experience of the early Christians than we imagine; for them also, unity was both a datum, as found in the one Lord, one faith, one baptism, and also a thing to be hoped, prayed and worked for. Sykes takes the principle of pluriformity so far as to describe Christianity not as a single religious group, but (as Hinduism is currently understood) as a 'family of religions with a common focus'. 'The complexity of describing the character of Christianity is not merely like that of describing the character of a single individual, but rather more like the task of discerning family likenesses in a large group of related individuals of different ages and stages of maturity.'[10]

'THE CURSE OF EVE'

Hardly have the lights of Epiphany been doused than we need to relight them for Candlemas (February 2nd), the Feast of the Purification of Mary, to which Bishop Cosin added the prefix 'The

Presentation of Christ in the Temple. The interval of 40 days was required by Jewish Law between the child's birthday and the day when the mother presented herself for readmission to the congregation and made her offering, both as thanksgiving for safe delivery and to 'dedicate' the child to God. We are allowed a glimpse of the performance by a poor Jewish family of their proper religious duties; they cannot afford the lamb, only the two pigeons, and they do not pay the customary five-shekel tax, because this child is not (Luke seems to imply) to be 'redeemed'; he 'belongs to the Lord' already, in a special way.

The Jewish notion that women need 'purification' after child-birth and before readmission to society seems to stem partly from the association of blood and birth with 'defilement'; partly from a close connection, made in widely different cultures and documented by Mary Douglas, between 'purity' and 'danger'.[11] In Jewish Law (Lev. 15) any bodily emission, from man or woman, brought 'uncleanness', and this has left its mark on subsequent associations between sexuality/intercourse/child-birth, on the one hand, and sin/impurity/guilt on the other. The text 'in sin did my mother conceive me' (Psalm 51, 5) has been widely used to associate sexual intercourse with sin. It seems rather to have referred to our common share in Original Sin, as the Jerusalem Bible has it:

> You know I was born guilty,
> a sinner from the moment of conception.

It should be set alongside the other Psalmist (127) who regarded child-birth as primarily a gift:

> Lo, children are an heritage of the Lord:
> And the fruit of the womb is his reward.

The pain of child-birth was widely considered to be part of 'the curse of Eve' (Gen. 3, 16); until well into the 19th Century the mother was expected to suffer and, until quite recently, suffer passively. In 1591 a midwife, Agnes Simpson, was burned at the stake for having attempted to relieve birth-pangs with opium or laudanum, one of many thousands of mid-wives, nurses and healers burnt as witches. Their crime was not in causing suffering but in endeavouring to relieve it. These 'wise women' practised as pharmacists, abortionists, nurses and midwives at a time when doctors and hospitals were not generally available and when the distinction between medicine and magic was a narrow one.[12]

While the stigma of 'pollution' has certainly been present in popular consciousness, it is thanksgiving that has been foremost in our own practice of 'Churching' after child-birth. The old 'Ordo ad Purificandem Mulierem post Partum' was entitled 'The Thanksgiving of Women after Child-Birth' in the 1662 BCP; and whereas previously this had been conducted at the church-door the mother was now invited to kneel at the communion-rail. It is perhaps significant that the ASB has replaced the 'churching' with a 'Service of Thanksgiving for the Birth of a Child': 'We thank you from our hearts for the life of this child, for a safe delivery, and for the privilege of parenthood.' The great advances in modern obstetrics have helped to remove references to 'the great pain and peril of child-birth'.

The custom of carrying candles in procession on Candlemas Day goes back to the earliest times. Alcuin in the 8th Century tells of crowds 'bearing a vast number of lights; and no one enters a public place in the city without a taper in his hand.' It recalls the Song of Simeon and his prophecy that the Child would prove 'a light to lighten the Gentiles.' This was the day when all the candles were blessed. Hency VIII ordered: 'On Candlemas Daye it shall be declared that the bearynge of candels is done to the memorie of Christe, the spirituall lyghte.' And later John Donne, Dean of St Paul's, approved the 'admitting of candles into the church because He Who was the Light of the Worlde was on this day of Lighte brought into the Temple of the Lord.' Snowdrops, appearing at this time, were called 'Mary's Tapers' or 'Candlemas Bells' and mark the beginning of the end of winter.[13]

> Candlemas come and gone,
> The snow lies on a hot stone.

As if the first spring flower was lifting a finger to test the temperature before it tries, with infinite daring, to cheat the rigours of Lent by beating Ash Wednesday to the draw.

NOTES

1. Thomas Hobbes, 'Leviathan', ch. 13.
2. See Roger Ruston, O.P., 'Apocalyptic and the Peace Movement', art. in New Blackfriars, May 1986, pp. 213–4, where he gives the sources both for 'born-again' and for non-Jewish Zionist apocalyptic. See also his 'Preparing for Armageddon', London Pax Christi, 1985, and an essay on 'The Apocalypse and the Peace Movement' by Andrew Chester in 'In God We Trust', London C.N.D., 1986.
3. Some commentators put the book much later and make the enemy the armies of Alexander the Great ('princes shall be a scorn unto them', 1.10). Possibly our present text is a rewriting of an earlier collection; the reference is different but the message is the same.
4. 'The Hermit of the Sahara' (1858–1916). He began life as a French cavalry officer, became first an explorer, then a Trappist. Called to the eremetical life, he established a hermitage in the Sahara where he was greatly revered but made no Moslem converts. He was assassinated by the Tuaregs in 1916, but his influence is still strong, mainly through the witness of the Little Brothers and Sisters of Father de Foucauld. See René Voillaume, 'Seeds of the Desert', London, 1955.
5. I have seen his like in pre-revolutionary Ethiopia when itinerant monks from distant monasteries would stand outside churches in the Capital (the modern 'Bethel') at the great Festivals, denouncing the sins of church and state with total impunity. However strict the limitations on free speech in what was undoubtedly a Police State, no one would have dared to touch them!
6. See Laurence Whistler, 'English Festivals', London 1947, p. 38. I am greatly indebted to this delightful book with its descriptions of traditional customs.
7. Oxford Book of Mystical Verse, 1932, p. 464.
8. See his 'Finality of Christ', London, 1969, p. 115, quoted in J.A.T. Robinson, 'The Human Face of God', London, 1973, p. 225, who adds his own comment: 'These claims are high enough in all conscience but they do not limit the mystery of the Christ to Jesus.' Robinson also quotes Raymond Panikkar as saying: 'Christ does not belong to Christianity, he only belongs to God' and comments: 'The finality or universality of Christ is not to be identified with the finality or universality of the Christian religion. In fact it would be nearer the truth to say that Christ is the "end" of Christianity as he is of Judaism – and that both positively and negatively' (p. 229).
9. See his article 'Christianity in a Pluralistic World – the economy of the Holy Spirit', Sobornost 6/3, 1971, pp. 166–74. How this works

out in missionary or evangelistic endeavour must surely depend on the particular encounter with a 'non-Christian' believer. It is encouraging to find the Dominican philosopher, Cornelius Ernst, ending his esay on 'The Necessity of the Church in the Context of Non-Christian Religions': 'After some communication prolonged into intimacy with some non-Christian, I may become sure that it is at least as likely that he is doing God's will as that I am; and I may make this sense the touchstone of my appreciation of the salutary efficacy of his religion and of other non-Christian religions. But that does not absolve me from the task of exhibiting in appropriate human terms just my sense of communication with my neighbour in Jesus Christ.' ('Multiple Echo', London, 1979, p. 223)

10. For a discussion of 'unity in pluriformity', see Stephen Sykes, 'Christian Theology Today', London, 1971, pp. 30–41.
11. See her 'Purity and Danger': an Analysis of Concepts of Pollution and Taboo', Routledge, 1966, p. 124. Douglas makes the connection between anxiety about the unity and integrity of the social group and concern to protect the body at its most vulnerable points. 'The Israelites were always in their history a hard-pressed minority . . . The threatened boundaries of their body politic would be well mirrored in their care for the integrity, unity and purity of the physical body.'
12. See Adrienne Rich, 'Of Woman Born', London, 1977, p. 128. She comments that 'the misogyny of the Church Fathers, which saw woman – especially her reproductive organs – as evil incarnate, attached itself to the birth-process, so that males were forbidden to attend at births, and the midwife was exhorted to make her primary concern not the comfort and welfare of the mother, but the baptism of the infant – in utero, with a syringe of holy water, if necessary.' (p. 134)
13. Whistler, op. cit., p. 87.

3

Spring into Summer

For love is crowned with the prime
In the spring time . . .
Sweet lovers love the spring.

If Spring comes, by common consent if not by change of temperature, with the Equinox or with March 25th and Lady Day, it could have no better herald than St. Valentine. Quite how this obscure Roman priest and 3rd Century martyr was enlisted to replace the Lupercalian orgy of ancient Rome is somewhat mysterious and possibly accidental. His day just happened to occur at the right time of year, in mid-Februry, and he filled a convenient niche. The custom of choosing a girl by lot to be a companion over the festivities, on the 'Paul Jones' principle, died hard: it became a game, subsequently relished by Samuel Pepys (Feb 14th, 1661), who took every advantage of the tradition whereby the first man or woman to be met that morning became your 'Valentine'.

THE LITTLE GOD

It was one way of baptising Eros (desire for the beloved) and ensuring that the little god had his rightful place in the Christian dispensation. He was not to be ousted by his equally powerful companions, Philia (friendship, mutuality) and Agape (self-giving love). Some have made such a sharp distinction between 'the two loves', spiritual and material, that they have been made to seem opposed and irreconcilable. 'Eros desires the good of the self', says M.C. D'Arcy, 'Agape is self-giving; Eros is man's way to God, Agape is God's way to man; Eros is the noblest form of egocentric love, Agape seeketh not its own; Eros seeks to gain its life by the possession of immortal beauty, Agape lives by God's life and therefore dares to lose its own. Eros is motivated by the beauty and value in the object, Agape bestows itself on what is quite unworthy, creates the value and is sovereign.'[1]

What are being analysed here are not two different 'things', entities, objects to be measured or categorised; but two different aspects of the self – myself as I am and myself as I would become. the distinction between love-as-desire and love-as-self-giving may provide a useful corrective for those who glibly imagine that 'all you need is Love'. Left to itself, unredeemed love may be possessive, egocentric, even destructive; in a culture hungry for love but saturated and obsessed with sexuality, it may be reduced to sensuality, an emotional 'whoosh', mere gut-response. It needs the action of grace if the self is to be transcended; otherwise, my dominant urge to self-fulfillment may lead me merely to exploit the other and treat him/her as an object, not as another subject.

In fact, the Bible makes no such sharp contrasts. As James Nelson observes, 'There is no separate word there (i.e. in the Greek Bible) for sexual love. "Agape" is used to describe the divine love, the intimate friendship of David and Jonathan, and the sensuous love of the Song of Songs alike . . . In short, this persisting dichotomy between Agape and Eros in so much Christian interpretation cannot be justified or explained by careful biblical and historical scholarship. The more likely reason for its pervasiveness is simply the pervasiveness of our experience of the alienating sexual dualisms.'[2]

When the Risen Christ gives his final absolution and commission to Peter (John 21, 15–18) he uses, in the language of the Fourth Gospel, the words Agapo and Philo without distinction. His question 'Do you love me (agapas)?' is answered by 'Yes, Lord, you know that I love you (philo).' His third question, however, uses Peter's word (phileis me). Similarly, in the Farewell Discourse, Jesus' great command to love (agapate) is followed by his calling them his 'friends' (philous). For St John, at least, the words seem to be interchangeable. He can speak of 'friendship' to describe our relationship with Christ or with each other: there is no hierarchy in love, but only mutuality in which both sexuality and altrusim cohere. 'If we define Christian love as agape or self-giving alone – without elements of desire, attraction, self-fulfilment, receiving – we are describing a love which is both impoverished and impoverishing. But the other elements of love without agape are ultimately self-destructive. Agape present with sexual desire, erotic aspiration and mutuality releases these from self-centredness and possessiveness into a relationship that is humanly enriching and creative. It does not annihilate or replace the other modes of our loving. It undergirds and transforms. And faith knows that agape is gift, and not of our own making.'[3]

St. Valentine must find his rightful place in our Christian Year. He stands for a true carnality; a proper measure of self-love; the unity of body, mind and spirit in our human response to God's gift of love. He prevents us from devaluing the sensual; being too high-minded; ignoring the sexual undercurrent in all relationships, even the most casual and 'innocent'. Like Puck, he points to a need for playfulness in a world where people invest too much in one-to-one relationships. 'Lord, what fools these mortals be', he laughs, puncturing our pride.

We are now poised to launch into the second great cycle of the Christian Year, based on Easter, beginning with Septuagesima. The mathematics behind the three Sundays before Lent is obscure. Some think the Seventy refers to the years of Israel's captivity in Babylon; but Christian writers have more naturally compared the Lenten fast (once called the Quadragesima) with the forty years spent wandering in the wilderness or Jesus' forty days in the desert of Temptation. However estimated, the 'Gesimas' provide a bridge between the light and joy of Epiphanytide and the solemnity of the weeks that prepare for Easter.

Their themes – 'Creation, Fall, Charity/Grace' – gave these weeks a natural shape and movement in the BCP. Their replacement in ASB by the themes: 'Christ the Teacher, the Healer, the Friend of Sinners' has its own rationale. It makes sense to begin this period with the Sower or the Sermon on the Mount and to end it with the Woman taken in Adultery. What better introduction to Shrove Tuesday than those authoritative words of absolution: 'Nor do I condemn you. You may go; do not sin again.' (John 8, 11)

DESIGN

Keble's contribution to Septuagesima is one of his rare hymns to have survived in general use:

There is a book, who runs my read,
  Which heavenly truth imparts,
And all the lore its scholars need,
  Pure lives and Christian hearts.

The works of God, above, below,
  Within us and around,
Are pages in that book, to show
  How God himself is found.

Certainly not as well known as his 'New Every Morning' or 'Blest are the Pure in Heart', it presents the Argument from Design in clear, straightforward terms. It echoes the Psalmist's 'The heavens declare the glory of God' and Hopkins' 'The world is charged with the grandeur of God'. Its tones are gentler, less grandiloquent and so, perhaps, more persuasive than Addison's in the previous Century:

The spacious firmament on high
With all the blue ethereal sky
And spangled heavens, a shining frame,
Their great Original proclaim . . .

Today our vision of the spacious firmament is obscured by the dust-clouds of Chernobyl, the mountains of unusable butter or surplus grain in the EEC or the piles of garbage which mean home for the shanty-dwellers of Lima or Mexico City. How do I dare speak of 'the works of an almighty hand' to a child born with brain-damage to a drug-addicted mother? We are denied the clarity and singleness of vision behind the Arab saying: 'I know there is a God – the same way I know when I see foot-prints in the sand that a traveller has passed this way.' It is not just that the world 'wears man's smudge and shares man's smell': not just that we have corrupted a creation that 'was very good'. Rather it appears itself to be flawed, imperfect; and our vision of it blurred by the impenetrable pain and anguish of innocent creatures.

It is the word Omnipotence – the work of an almighty hand – that sticks in the throat. If we must speak of God's 'Power' as we do of his Love and Justice, it is of quite a different order from power as it is commonly wielded or experienced in the world. In that (the world's) sense we should rather say with Berdyaev that 'God has less power than a policeman'.[5] It can only be bracketed with Love and Justice if it is seen as limited by them, or at least self-limited. In the light of the Gospels the Almighty Hand is seen not as a clenched fist, the symbol of power for those who see it coming from the barrel of a gun, but as the open hand, pierced, helpless and pinioned to a Cross. If we take the Gospels seriously we have to see power embodied not in Pilate, but in the prisoner who stands bound before him, of whom we say both 'Ecce Homo' and 'Ecce Deus'. It is only when we have come to terms with the power and powerlessness of the everlasting arms that we can, without distorting Love and Justice, claim to 'discern God's hand in all his works'.

All descriptions of God's grandeur in creation are simply pictures, images, and we are rightly told to beware of images. Words can be as idolatrous as images – even the word 'God', unless we remember that 'behind God is God': 'This is Thou, yet is not this Thou'. The value of the creation-stories lies in their central affirmation that God has said Yes to his world – at its heart it is still 'very good'. The N.T. goes further: it affirms (only once, but at least once!) that God actually loves his world. It is that kind of 'Yes'. More than that, he is in some mysterious way identified with it: with the smudge and smell, blear, smear, soil and toil of it. If 'generations have trod, have trod . . . ' then God, in Christ, has trod it too: not just 'in the garden in the cool of the day', but in the sweaty agony of the garden of Gethsemane. And if we must call him 'Almighty' and speak of his 'Power', it is the power to unite and heal a divided, alienated world: the power not to bring down Pilate, but to forgive and raise up Peter.

DISEASE

It is this power to heal and forgive that provides the theme for the next week, Sexagesima. 'Ransomed, healed, restored, forgiven . . .' In those words lies the kernel of Christian Gospel. In this highly complex creature, homo sapiens, we are only just beginning to appreciate the subtle interrelation of mind, body and spirit: 'disease' points to their dissociation or disharmony on the one hand and their alienation from the environment on the other.

The causes of that alienation lie partly in the 'cracked vase' of creation itself: the groaning and travailing that Paul speaks of in Romans 8. Partly, also, in the mystery of human freedom which Berdyaev made the corner-stone of his philosophy and theodicy.[6] He distinguishes three kinds of freedom. (1) That which is rooted in God himself who can choose to create, love and even destroy his creation. (2) The freedom that makes us truly human, 'la gloire et le rébut de l'univers', capable of both heights and depths, from Beethoven to Buchenwald. (3) The freedom which presents a mystery comparable to the mystery of evil itself. For Berdyaev, they belong together and cannot be separated. What we call 'Satan' is the manifestation of irrational freedom at its deepest level, part of the reality along which we humans travel. Being human, created with free will, we are bound to disobey, act contrary to our true nature and our ultimate good. And the drama of our inner conflict, the 'war of the members', is reflected also in cosmic terms, in spiritual reality, 'the War in Heaven'.

If the causes of our dis-ease (sickness, sin, alienation, however it is presented) are mysterious, so also is its cure. Questions like: Why do we become 'ill'? What brings on migraine? What causes cancer? touch depths which anatomy and physiology cannot reach. We know that we can to some degree control our own sickness: we can encourage a headache when it is convenient and on occasion stay on our feet to face a crisis. Stress, a 'body-blow' like losing a job or a near relative may be a trigger, a constituent cause of cancer; break-down may be of the body or the mind – or both.

Similarly, any reversal or alleviation of the symptoms may derive from a complex variety of factors, including the will of the patient and the attitude (supportive, optimistic, caring) of those around him. Clearly, 'health' is not to be equated with 'being (or feeling well'. It is not just 'how I am in myself'; but how I am relating to others, at home or at work.

In the Gospels we find Jesus healing people almost in spite of himself; almost wearily ('except you see signs and wonders you will not believe'), when such cures were seen as evidence of supernatural powers, not as 'signs of the Kingdom'. Granted the mysterious combination of circumstances that attends any 'healing', it is not surprising that each instance is different. Sometimes the cooperation of the patient – faith, desire for healing, positive thinking – is required; sometimes simply the cooperation of friends like the stretcher-bearers on behalf of the paralytic (Matt. 9, 2–8; Mark 2, 5); some are healed beyond their wildest dreams and expectations, while for others he can do nothing. Jesus clearly perceived the association of sickness with 'sin' and yet refused to accept the idea that sickness and disability were in any sense 'God's judgment' (John 9, 3). His characteristic action was to restore the patient to his/her community, to make them at one not just in themselves but with their environment.

In the life and experience of the early Christians, healing was a sign of the New Age: a feature of their community life that demanded their prayers and intimate concern. There was no magic about it. Those who, like Simon Magus (Acts 8, 1919, thought that there was some magical, supernatural power to be captured and exploited were severely discouraged. Jesus, we may infer from the narrative of the Temptations, was open to the possibility of using miraculous demonstrations as a way of convincing and converting people, but rejected it as a manipulative invasion of human freedoms. His 'cup' of suffering was not removed at Gethsemane and would in the future, he said, be shared by his followers and friends: Paul's 'thorn in the flesh' (eye-trouble? epilepsy?) was never removed, as far as we know. This does not mean that we have to accept whatever is handed out to us with stoical fatalism – God, who wills that 'all things work together for good', wills our 'good' also: that we should be whole, integrated people, cooperating and responding freely and with full consent.

The process of healing means essentially aligning ourselves to that will, cooperating with it and not, as we well may, frustrating it. And that not merely for ourselves, but for others. Praying for the sick can be an arduous, even dangerous activity if accompanied by real faith, hope and a readiness to be used, at whatever cost, as the means of another's well-being. To 'wish another well' may mean to become transparent to God's healing power, allowing it to flow through us to another. Because in our arrogance or lack of faith we think we know God's will for that person before we have even begun to pray, the natural tendency is to 'hope' for too little or too much. 'No one in this world ever loved too much,' said Traherne,[7] 'but only in a wrong way, and all in too short a measure.' To avoid that 'wrong way' it may help to follow some well-tried guidelines:

- Choose a particular symptom or weakness to pray about and concentrate on that (Blake's 'minute particulars', not 'the general good');
- Let your prayer dwell not on the continuing trouble, but on the healed condition;
- Focus your imagination on what you actively desire and ask that this may be within God's will;
- Always thank God for the power that makes us 'whole', even if it does not (apparently or immediately) make us 'well'.

For all its indeterminacy, we are acutely aware of the toughness and stubborn intractibility of matter. However fearfully and wonderfully made, the body is still St. Francis' Brother Ass which persists in going against, not with, the grain. Nevertheless, it is still the vehicle for the action of God's healing Spirit, more than we ask or know. In the end, all we can do is put ourselves within the Will, in every circumstance; to be still, open, sensitive, single-minded and wait, aware that God has all our destinies in his hands . . .

> I would be still, sensitive, a winged gift . . . (D.H. Lawrence)
> There is one whose hands this universal falling
> can't fall through . . . (Rilke)

Then I can pray 'deliver us' from this particular evil, this pain; and say with Augustine: 'All my hope is nowhere but in your exceeding great mercy. Give what you command and command what you will' (Da quod jubes et jube quod vis). Or, to paraphrase the incomparable words of Wesley's Covenant Service: 'I am no longer my own, but yours. Put me to what you will; put me to doing, put me to suffering; I freely and heartily yield all things to your pleasure and disposal.'

Because the healing-process is so complex it may also be long and, like forgiveness, painful. If there is no 'cheap grace' there is no 'cheap therapy' either. What is the 'I' that looks for healing and integration? This mass of competing, conflicting emotions, desires, forces for good or evil – or the calm, unruffled, positive 'I' that outstares its reflection in the shaving-mirror? It is not just 'I' who needs to be healed; but my shadow-self, the past with its memories and unfinished business, the future with its anxieties, the fears that paralyse my will to act, holding me rigid as a rabbit, locked in a car's headlamps. Whoever 'I' am, I don't particularly like it, so I am tempted to punish it (masochism) or try to be rid of it (escapism).

> Nothing (says Donne) of all invenomed things
> Doth work upon itself, with inborne stings.

Because I cannot accept my self 'just as I am', I find it hard to believe that anyone else can unreservedly accept me. Then I read: 'Not that we loved him, but that he loved us' and know that at the heart of this mysterious Christian truth I am or can be 'acceptable'. It is the hardest but most necessary truth I can encounter, but it is the best news mankind ever received.

In the end I know that it is the love that casts out fear that can release me for effective action. I am caught up in this healing process when I can accept the truth about myself and know that I am acceptable as I am, warts and all, with all the conflicts and inconsistencies. By being shown what Love means I am enabled to love, to accept others as I have myself been accepted. I have listened to the tune of that 'other song' and can learn, as I could in no other way, to sing it for myself.

FRIENDSHIP

At first sight, the tune seems a simple one, as if we were invited to sing 'All you need is Love' or cultivate what Bertrand Russell called 'kindly feelings'. The third pier in the bridge that leads us over to Lent invites us, at Quinquagesima, to explore not just the experience of love, but also the mystery of faith and the offer of grace: the harmonies that undergird the tune. What is presented is nothing less than the Friendship of Christ himself, extended to all and sundry without discrimination, like those hands outstretched on the Cross to embrace the world.

It is significant that this new relationship, corresponding to the 'new commandment', should be recorded only by the Fourth Gospel which has uniquely emphasised God's love for the world. Rabbis would not ordinarily think of their pupils as 'friends': this one was addressed in polite fashion as Teacher or 'Sir' (Kyrie). No doubt they would continue to do so, but now he proclaims a new status and invites them to a closer intimacy: 'No longer do I call you servants (doulous), for the servant does not know his master's mind. But I have called you friends (philous), for all that I have heard from the Father I have made known to you' (John 15, 15). As Paul was confidently, triumphantly to affirm, 'We have the mind of Christ.'

There may be an echo here of Abraham's designation as 'God's friend' (2 Chron. 20, 7) or of God talking to Moses as a man talks with his friend' (Exod. 33, 11). It was a commonplace amongst Greek thinkers that the wise are God's friends: 'Pas sophos theou philos' – every wise man is a friend of God (a Stoic saying). This would certainly have been familiar to Christ's contemporaries, at least through the Wisdom literature and passages like Wisdom 7, 22–27: ' . . . She (Wisdom) makes all things new: and in all ages entering into holy souls she makes them friends of God and prophets.' 'For she is a treasure to men that never fails: which they that use become the friends of God, being commended for the gifts that come from learning' (7, 14). Now, however, the new friendship is based not merely on knowing the Truth but on doing it – keeping the word, the new commandment.

If we are ever tempted to sentimentalise the idea of the Friendship of Christ ('There's a friend for little children', 'My master and my friend' etc.), we should remember that the offer of friendship is conditional, dependent on our response not simply to the host but to our fellow-guests, the least of his brothers and sisters. The response is moral, not emotional: love and obedience are closely intertwined, and we are required to become ourselves, as Samaritan counsellors describe themselves, 'befrienders'. Those who first heard those words 'you are my friends' had learned the meaning when the Master washed their feet.

Experience of human friendship, 'begotten of sympathy and fed by opportunity', gives us the clue to the mysterious, vine-and-branches Friendship 'in Christ' into which the believer is invited to enter, when we will the ultimate good of the other as he wills ours. Cicero spoke of 'an active and disinterested desire for the welfare of someone who returns that love in equal measure.' No passage in our own literature extols this more beautifully than Jeremy Taylor's Discourse on Friendship. 'After all this, treat thy friend kindly, love to be with him, do to him all the worthinesses of love and fair endearment, according to thy capacity and his; bear with his infirmities till they approach towards being criminal; but never dissemble with him, never despise him, never leave him. Give him gifts and upbraid him not, and refuse not his kindnesses, and be sure never to despise the smallness or the impropriety of them . . . Friendship is the allay of our sorrows, the ease of our passions, the discharge of our oppressions, the sanctuary of our calamities, the counsellor of our doubts, the exercise and improvement of what we meditate.'

This applies as much to our Friendship with Christ as to our human friendships. Neither are earned – they remain a gift and a grace, not to be grabbed or taken for granted, but to be 'kept in constant repair'; cultivated, strengthened even by times of conflict and disagreement; even by physical separation. We are given a glimpse of the withdrawal-pains that awaited Mary Magdalene if she was to exchange the old familiar friendship with the Master for a new and closer relationship with her Living Lord. Those words: 'Noli me tangere' were not a rebuff, a turn-off, but an invitation to grow such as a patient has to work through in relationship with the analyst if he is to move through 'transference' to independence.

A true understanding of the meaning of friendship, such as we find in Jeremy Taylor or, earlier, in Cicero, Augustine or Aelred of Rievaulx, has no room for a sentimentality where possessiveness frustrates growth. It remains an art, with all the care and discipline that true art requires. We can demand too much or too little of it: we can refuse to allow our friends to grow away, especially if they are also our children. It is always true that the good is the enemy of the best: corruptio optimi pessima. There is no sense of betrayal like that of a friend who expects, as Freud did from Jung, complete understanding and absolute loyalty. Honesty, integrity and truth itself refuse to reduce friendship to mere collusion.

'Reduced to its simplest terms,' writes John Burnaby, 'the existence of love in a human being means that the eye of the spirit has opened to the sunshine of good. A man has seen that which is good, and seeing it has delighted in it. His delight is acceptance, and what is accepted is a gift; he must ask who is the giver and why should anything have been given to *him*. The only answer to that question is love. He *sees* that the gift of good can be nothing but the expression of love, and that love itself is greater than any or all of the gifts in which its activity is displayed. If greater, then more to be desired; and if he can desire above all things the gift of love, if he can truly cast out of his heart all that is contrary to love, then love will be given to him, and he will have power to return it to the giver. In such fruition of a supreme good there is supreme delight, and the delight itself is radiant, 'diffusive of itself', creative.'[8]

This is surely the litmus test for our life as the People of God and our commitment both to each other, bearing one another's burdens, and also to our service of the world. To call ourselves a 'Family' requires further definition; the N.T. speaks of 'household' rather than 'family'. For Paul, 'family' denotes 'human family' (as in Eph. 3, 15), the patria of all who call God 'pater'. The 'household of faith' (oikeioi, Gal. 6, 10) or 'of God' (Eph. 2, 19) approximate more closely to our 'extended family' than to the narrower, nuclear family with its clannishness and possessiveness. To use the word of Christian groups and congregations may only serve to make others feel excluded, if their own experience of family is one of rejection – not belonging. To see ourselves primarily as a 'Company of Friends', with all the moral demands that this entails, ensures that we remain open and not closed to the world. We can never share the Gospel if we are not prepared to share the gift of friendship and make of others what Christ has made of us, his friends.

From quiet homes and small beginnings
  Out to the undiscovered ends,
There's nothing worth the wear of winning
  But laughter and the love of friends.

OPENNESS

The first demand we make of a friend is honesty – that he should 'open with us'; for without the capacity to speak (and listen to) the truth in love no one and certainly no friendship can grow. To have someone, man or woman, to whom anything can be said without concealment or demur; who can assure us that nothing, not even murder, if faced and not concealed under a blanket of self-delusion (the sin against the Spirit, presumably), is in the last resort unforgivable; to allow at least one person to see us as, in the heart's confession, we see ourselves – this is a basic human need. Shrove Tuesday points to it and the discipline of confession/absolution celebrates it. Never widely, in a formal way, practised by Anglicans under that generous dispensation: 'All may, some should, nobody must.' But the shriving of friends – and of husband and wife in friendship – is for many the beginning of wisdom and the gateway to self-knowledge. We do not have to resort to the pretentious language of 'counselling' to recognise that the need and the opportunity are available to all.

No poem has unlocked the secrets of the human heart more profoundly than the one we know as Pslam 139, 'Domine, Probasti Me'. It carries us into the presence of Truth and drives us deeper into the mystery of selfhood, what it means to be human: 'Look within and find God.' In its majestic sweep it carries us from the dark recesses of our inner being into the awesome light of truth: it acknowledges the evil around and within, but points through it to 'the way everlasting'.

The poet leads us in through our common experience of creatureliness. I am known by the one 'to whom all hearts are open, all desires known and from whom no secrets are hid' – the Artist and Architect, the Potter who works in clay. I am his flawed masterpiece and if I claim to be original I am only thinking his thoughts after him. My sense of creaturehood corresponds to my overriding sense of his omnipotence: the mystery of the 'shekinah' whose centre is everywhere and circumference nowhere. His Spirit can breathe on the waters of my inner chaos and create order, renewing me as he renews the face of the earth.

Part of me rebels and wishes to evade this relentless omniscience. Hounded by faith and sometimes hindered by theology, I resent the probings of conscience. Like Adam in the garden, I want to hide: perhaps walls (v.4) round the self would help? But still I am pursued, even besieged, and part of me resists this 'battering of my heart':

> I like an usurped towne to another due
> Labour to admit you, but Oh, to no end . . .

I cannot build walls against the truth, for the truth is within the self, so 'fearfully and wonderfully made'.

And so the Psalmist returns to the mystery of his own

creatureliness, his sense of being uniquely made and loved (v.12), the greatest mystery of all. There is purpose and design if only we can read the Author's book, in which our every thought is recorded (v.15). He holds us in his hand as Dame Julian held the tiny hazelnut:

'I looked thereupon with eye of my understanding, and thought: "What may this be?" And it was answered generally thus: "It is all that is made." I marvelled how it might last, for methought it might suddenly have fallen to nought for littleness. And I was answered in my understanding: "It lasteth, and ever shall last for that God loveth it." And so All-thing hath the Being by the love of God.

'In this Little Thing I saw three properties. The first is that God made it, the second is that God loveth it, the third that God keepeth it.'[9]

But if I am unique then so necessarily is everyone else! All humankind (the Greek text says 'all men', not 'all members') are written in the Book. Not just God's 'friends' but his 'enemies' also. It is at this point in the poem that there is a change of key; as if all the poet's suppressed animosity, feelings of anger, hurt, fear, persecution rise to the surface and erupt in a blaze of indignation. It is the anger of Theresa of Avila who, on one of her more rigorous journeys got stuck in a river and lost a wheel from her carriage. She got out in the pouring rain, looked up and shook her fist: 'No wonder, Lord, you have so few friends when you treat them like this!' This poet writes as a member of a small oppressed group surrounded by hostile nations, men of violence (v.19). Perhaps, like the writer of Psalm 137, he is seated 'by the waters of Babylon', longing to return home. Like the prophets before him who attacked the exploitativeness of those who are 'deceitful on the weights' and 'sell the needy for a pair of shoes', he gives full expression to his anger at the gross injustice of it all.

Not to admit one's anger, to repress it and allow ourselves to be silently 'consumed' by it is both dangerous and damaging. A cancer patient has to be encouraged to articulate his anger and so prevent the cancer and the anger feeding on, 'eating up' the patient. Our natural response to news of some appalling injustice is one of outrage – 'How dare they . . . ?' – and the pity of it is that most of us are not angry enough. We are not impelled to action, or the anger merely melts into a soured bitterness and a sense of impotence. 'Too often,' says Frances Wilson, 'we, the Church, look at bitterness and tell people to stop being angry. I think that is wrong. We must focus on the impotence and ask how this can be transformed so that the anger itself can be a cleansing and renewing energy as it was in the case of our Lord.'[10]

Facing one's anger and if necessary expressing it, as the Psalmist does, may be the first step to therapy and positive action. Anger can be not a negative reaction but the trigger-mechanism that releases the possibility of new growth: a spur to action and a challenge to change. 'To ask if one's anger in some issue is really necessary is a challenge to what one is and so it can be seen as a threat, even though it may actually mean putting one's foot on the first rung of the ladder of a new happiness.'[11] To receive the anger of another and absorb it is both a punishment and a privilege, shared as much by M.P.s, social workers and bank managers as by doctors and hospital chaplains.

Our Psalmist makes no attempt to 'spiritualise' the antagonism he feels. But he recognises the danger of all 'righteous indignation' if he claims to be on the Lord's side and falls victim to holier-than-thou arrogance or presumption. And so his final prayer is for self-knowledge; he asks to be sifted, 'proved' (the word is that used for the testing of metals), examined (as in school or a court of law) and directed away from Anomie and ineffective righteous indignation, in the way of eternal life. Sifting and proving the secrets at 'the deep heart's core' make the keeping of Lent not a burden but a means of discovery and new growth.

DISCIPLINE & DELIGHT

Fasting and feasting have always chased each other round the year, like the Lion and the Unicorn round about the town, mutually necessary and inseparable. Like Plato's Charioteer, we have to keep the two horses together, in balance; the pancakes and the penitence of Shrove Tuesday both remind us of the rigours to come with what George Herbert called – and welcomed – as 'deare Feast of Lent.' With the mandatory finishing up of the butter and lard went the romps of street-football, the pancake races through the town, customs taken over (like the Lupercalia of Epiphany) from the old Roman Empire.

Yet Lord instruct us to improve our fast
By starving sinne and taking such repast,
As may our faults controll:
That every man may revell at his doore,
Not in his parlour; banquetting the poore,
And among those his soul.[12]

The word 'Lent' itself is probably derived from the old English word for Spring, Lencten, the time when, the long nights past, the days mercifully lengthen. From the earliest times (the custom was well established by the 2nd Century), the forty days before Easter were kept as a period of special training and particular ascetic practices, though the manner and timing varied in the different traditions. It was a time when catechumens were prepared for baptism at Easter; and St Chrystostom speaks of some who took only bread and water throughout Lent and others who abstained even from that for two days in the week. The Orthodox have always observed the fast most rigidly and include even Sundays, contrary to the practice in other churches, as fast-days.

In spite of relaxations arising out of World War II and rationing, there may be new insights into the value of fasting in our time. Firstly, the unity of body/mind/spirit has been emphasised by Eastern spirituality which has served to correct Western tendencies to dualism. The state of the body, posture in prayer, our acceptance of the body's own special contribution to the well-being of the whole person, our incarnational approach to 'embodiment' have all helped to correct a 'bias against the body' which has characterised some Western spirituality.

Secondly, we have been forced by our awareness of the needs of the hungry and the real possibility of world famine to think more deeply about our own eating habits, balanced diet and the perils of obesity. While for some this degenerates into mere 'food-fetishism' and an obsession with eating/not eating to the point of anorexia, this leads others to appreciate the value of fasting and healthy abstinence as a discipline to enlighten the senses and sharpen awareness.

Thirdly, we have learned from many different sources the importance of body-language. It provides a necessary means of communication not only between people but also in political dialogue and action. No one knew this better than Gandhi. He fasted to evoke the good that was always latent in people, to appeal to their better motives. In his efforts to develop Hindu–Moslem friendship he found that nothing else worked. 'Nothing evidently which I say or write can bring the two communities together,' he declared. 'I fasted to reform those who loved me.' It was his way of touching their hearts and demonstrating the gravity of the crisis that demanded from them, too, a way of renunciation. At the time of his death, when he had agreed to break his final fast, he seemed to have been successful. Where words had failed, that tiny, frail, emaciated body had, for a time at least, averted catastrophe.[13]

Lastly, we are learning and shall be called upon to learn more of the importance of simplifying, 'living simply that others may simply live'. More may not mean worse, but less may certainly mean richer. A visitor to the National Gallery has a world of aesthetic treasure at his disposal; richer at that moment than the tycoon who has bought a rare Rembrandt. To be released from relentless acquisitiveness is to be poor, yet making many rich: penniless, but owning the world.

> A loaf of bread, the walrus said, is what we chiefly need –
> Pepper and vinegar besides are very nice indeed . . .

It is the way of true wisdom to differentiate the loaf from the clutter of condiments that may conceal and not enhance its true flavour.

So, on Ash Wednesday, with the simplest, starkest symbolism, the body is marked with dust, the visible sign of mortality and penitence. 'Remember, O man, that dust thou art and unto dust shalt thou return.' As if to complete the cycle of seasons, last year's Palms become this year's ashes. In our day we are spared the terrible curses and denunciations of the 'Commination Service' (or 'denouncing of God's anger and judgments against sinners') which survives only in the singing of Psalm 51 in the liturgy, sometimes to the magical music of Allegri. It may yet merit revival, to give some an opportunity to recite 'Cursed is he who removeth his neighbour's landmark' outside the Stock Exchange; and others 'Cursed is he that putteth his trust in man and taketh man for his defence' at the doors of the Ministry of Defence.

All three Synoptic accounts of Jesus' own Forty Days take him straight from his Jordan-baptism to the desert. 'Full of Holy Spirit' he is led by the Spirit to have his vocation tested and is left vulnerable, exposed, hungry, alone, to wrestle with his conscience and his God. It is as if we were being shown in a dramatic way the necessary connection between the way of commitment and the way of the Cross. 'Are you able to be baptised with my baptism?' 'We are.' 'You shall.' Is it not strange, then, that we should be told to pray every day that this should not happen to us? 'Lead us not . . . ' Even granted the Jewish way of ascribing everything that happens to the hand of God: granted a better sense might be 'Do not allow us to be stretched beyond our limits' (since 'God will not allow you to be tempted above that ye are able' – 1 Cor. 10, 13): it still seems strange that we should ask not be taken, whatever the cost, where he unmistakably led.

The word 'Peirasmos' itself has baffled translators so effectively that after flirting with 'the time of trial', 'the ordeal' (Rieu), 'hard testing' (TEV), 'the test' (Jerusalem Bible), we have been sent back to 'Temptation' and told to make the best we can of it. The testing of cars, metals and applicants for jobs is a necessary process to be undergone, if not exactly enjoyed. As with the 'little deaths' these tests prepare us for the crunch-point which may come later when we are ready and strong enough to meet it. That, surely, is a legitimate prayer. As the French translation has it, 'Et ne nous laissez pas succomber à la tentation.' It is John Donne's prayer:

> I have a sin of fear, that when I've spun
>   My last thread, I shall perish on the shore;
> Swear by thyself that at my death thy Sun
>   Shall shine as it shines now, and heretofore;
>   And having done that, thou hast done,
>   I have no more.

There is also an undercurrent to the prayer, a hint of a final crisis – persecution, loss of a life-partner, moments when we shall need special strength and protection. The NT writers expected a final struggle, a time of affliction ('thlipsis', a word much used by Simone Weil) which would precede the End. The writer of the Letters to the Seven Churches of Asia promises 'Because thou didst keep the word of my patience, I also will keep thee from the hour of trial (peirasmou), that hour which is to come upon the whole world, to try them that dwell upon the earth' (Rev. 3, 10). Our prayer recalls this promise, as if we were to pray for deliverance not just from war but from the effects of war. The last two clauses of the Lord's Prayer are inseparable.

It would be the height of presumption to imagine that we could ever reconstruct the thought-processes presented to us in symbolical form as the Temptation-Story. What we read is, presumably, the 'disclosure-event' as it was recounted to the Twelve in terms intelligible to anyone familiar with the Book of Job. What is undeniable is, firstly, that the 'exposure' to the powers of evil was deliberate and not accidental. However we interpret 'the Evil One' of the Lord's Prayer, it corresponds to a reality which Jesus confronted throughout his life. To be confronted by the power of 'diminishment' is to choose between surrender ('fall down and worship') and walking taller.

Secondly, the choices presented are not between good and evil but between two goods: Jesus is tested at the point not of his weaknesses but of his strengths. All the choices must have been real possibilities: to allow the good to supersede the best – settle, in fact, for second best: to use doubtful means (supernatural power) to serve a desirable end: and to take the short-cut of compulsion and the invasion of human freedom to inaugurate the Kingdom. Here, and not for the last time, 'the last temptation is the greatest treason, to do the right thing for the wrong reason.'

It is now clear why it is the Spirit that drives Jesus into the desert. All the tests are of love, by love. The fact of love was not in doubt: only its quality could be diminished and its methods distorted. 'Love wove the shirt of flame . . . ' and at the end of it all, as a result of any good prayer, there is heightened awareness and greater sensitivity to the direction of the Spirit. From Jordan, through the desert to the proclamation of the first Manifesto in the synagogue at Nazareth the Spirit moves, guides and impels.

This is the sense in which we can say with George Herbert: 'Welcome deare Feast of Lent!' The Spirit drives us out to do battle with the power of diminishment in its characteristic forms – cynicism, disenchantment and despair. We are told that during his Lent 'angels ministered to Jesus', which we might vulgarly translate as: 'He got the message' – he could detect a meaning behind it all, and the meaning and the message saw him through. As Hans Kung has said: 'The believer knows no way of avoiding suffering, but he knows a way through it.'

THE GREEN YEARS

If Lent, like Spring itself, brings growth, it will also bring its own growing-pains; 'shades of the prison-house begin to fall upon the growing boy'. Adolescence, in the green years of our own Spring, brings the most intense conflicts: the awakening of new drives and passions sharpens the pleasures of meeting and the agonies of parting. Just as there is no joy like the discovery of another and mutual acceptance 'in depth', so there is no pain like that of a first real love-affair when its end seems like the end of the world. To love, as the Greeks said, is to suffer, and for the adolescent there is a very thin line between the ecstacies of the Saints and the torments of the damned. It is ironical, yet understandable, that there is no time when the death-wish is so strong; we are strangely prone to suicide not when our powers are failing, but when they are at their peak.

Internal conflicts are accentuated by growing tensions seething into open conflict with family and society. Ideas, tastes (not least in music!) and values are common sources of intergenerational conflict. Social and economic deprivation sharpen it; the young may not be able to flee the family nest when they should; the addition of ageing, possibly senile grand-parents makes a two-tier family into a three-tier cage. Yet to cut the umbilical, pack a hold-all and run – perhaps straight into the arms of a parent-substitute – brings further anxiety. Fear of freedom and emotional independence induces feelings of guilt. The young fear to take control and their parents to lose it, and with it their perceived role of guardian and guide. 'They (adolescents) are classical demonstrations,' writes Jack Dominian, 'of the failure to possess themselves minimally and at a time when society has decided that they must control their own destiny with the minimum of external support (such as army service, apprenticeship or supervision); far from being drop-outs they are still waiting to enter, to drop into their identity . . . It is not surprising that this age-group (16–18) has the highest marital breakdown rate.'[14]

Conflict arises out of difference and is inherent in our humanity. As Noel Coward sang, 'When Eve said to Adam: Start calling me madam, The world grew far more exciting': it also became fraught with necessary conflict. Eden brought alienation and also, East of Eden, Cain. So the drama unfolds; the 'scandal of particularity' brings conflict between Jew and Gentile, the Christian and 'the world'. Our Judaeo-Christian story is one of struggle and continuing conflict. Jacob wrestles with his brother, then with the Angel; Joseph is alienated from his people; Job and Elijah, the great patriarchs and prophets, argue with God as fiercely as they denounce the Establishment; Jesus, like the Baptist before him, invites criticism as warmly as he denounces the critics.

CONFLICT & CONFRONTATION

The Fourth Gospel in particular contains passages of the fiercest invective and most violent denunciations of the unfortunate Pharisees – much of it giving a biased picture of contemporary Judaism. The seeds of the anti-semitism that has stained the pages of our subsequent history are to be traced back to these Gospel sources. A saying like 'You are of your father the Devil' (John 8, 44) tells us more about the conflict between the infant Church and its Jewish parents than it does of the disagreements between Jesus and his fellow-rabbis.

Nevertheless, he states as a defined objective: 'I have come to set fire to the earth . . . to bring not peace but a sword . . . ' (Matt. 10, 34) . . . 'to set sons against fathers, daughters against mothers.' Can this be the Christ of the Beatitudes speaking? The whole context within which the Gospel is proclaimed is one of conflict and struggle. The heroic resistance of the Maccabees, nationalist movements like the Zealots or the Sicarii, welcomed even into the inner core of the movement in the persons of Simon and (probably) Judas; the continuing struggle to maintain Jewish customs and identity in the teeth of colonial oppression; the presence of different factions within the Jewish hierarchy itself (Sadducees, Herodians etc.) – all these ensured that Palestine was a barbed-wire minefield many centuries before the Mandate and the Six Day War.

A MORE EXCELLENT WAY

Given such a religio-political climate, confrontation was inevitable: but it did not necessarily mean becoming an instrument or instigator of further violence – that was the way Jesus explicitly rejected in the desert and at the last in the Garden of Gethsemane ('They that take the sword shall perish by the sword'). It seems likely that the (hardly non-violent) expulsion of the traders from the Temple should be placed at the beginning, where John has it, not at the end of the Ministry. If so, it may well represent a time when the 'more excellent way' of suffering love and the Servant theme had not yet been fully developed. What may provide an intermediate stage is the incident (John 6) when he is apparently invited to lead a popular revolt; the people want to take him by force and make him a kind of Fidel Castro. His response is to slip quietly away and retreat into the hills.

In each of the Gospels this follows the mysterious Feeding of the Multitude. They are, in Mark's words (6, 34) as sheep without a shepherd or, in another sense, 'looking for leadership', an army without a general. Is Jesus to be another Joshua? In John's account, this is no ordinary teaching- or healing-mission; he arranges the people (they are mostly or entirely men) by ranks, in quasi-military fashion. Hugh Montefiore points out that the event is preceded by the death of the Baptist and suggests a massive demonstration of his followers who wish to take over the new movement and avenge their martyred leader.[15] 'From the days of John the Baptist until now, the Kingdom suffers violence and violent men try to capture it.' (Matt. 11, 12). Only a hypothesis, perhaps, but it is significant that Jesus responds by conducting a kind of Eucharist, teaching them about the Bread of Life and showing them what, rightly understood, can be the most subversive and revolutionary action we know: the Sacrament of the more excellent way – giving, blessing, breaking and sharing. Whether disenchanted by this strange teaching or disappointed at his failure to meet their nationalist aspirations, many withdraw at this point and leave the movement. The first prophecy of the Passion almost immediately follows (Mark 8, 31).

In fact, this seems to have been the crunch-point, the dividing-line, between those who followed the accepted Messianic party-line and those who, with whatever reservations (and we know how little even the inner core had understood 'the mind of Christ'), were prepared to attempt the more excellent way. It has been so down the ages. Just as many of Gandhi's followers in post-Independence India have found the principle of Satyagraha idealistic and impractical, unsuitable to a world governed by realpolitick; so many Christians have either misunderstood the way of the Cross or have found it too demanding. The Church has been tempted to use worldly power to gain its ends – by the Crusades, the Inquisition or by oppressive legislation like the Codes of Justinian and Clarendon. The Church of England has used 'Establishment' to exclude non-members – Catholics, Jews, Independents – from Universities and positions of influence ('Subscription No Bondage!'). On occasion it has tried to manipulate public opinion, through fear of anarchy or the Communist Conspiracy, to bolster the forces of law and order and reinforce social control. It has sided with those in positions of privilege to foment fear of external forces, impose repressive authority and prevent freedom of speech and dissent.

'But it shall not be so amongst you.' 'He that is not with me is against me.' The more excellent way is bound to be different, difficult and incalculably dangerous. It is paradoxical that Gandhi, the man of non-violence, should have met a violent death at the hands of one of his own people because he threatened the status quo of Hindu supremacy. Paradoxical, too, that Jesus met his violent death at the hands of his own people in collusion with the colonial power because he threatened the religious and political authorities of his day. Caiaphas spoke more truly than he knew when he charged the prisoner (as Socrates in his turn was charged) with 'perverting the people'. Conflict and contentiousness could only end in what has always symbolised them, a +: but for 'followers in the Way' that is a symbol not merely of conflict and division but also of forgiveness and reconciliation.

CROSS-TALK

Our own culture has been so thoroughly saturated with cross-symbolism that is hard to experience the shock, the intolerable affront to accepted tradition and historical expectation, which it must have inflicted on an unsuspecting world. To E.M. Forster's 'Only Connect' we have to add: 'Only Contextualise'. If it was hard enough to digest this new truth that 'the Son of Man must suffer', it was harder still to find that 'if they have persecuted me they will persecute you also'. When training, instinct, even Scripture itself combine to reinforce an association of suffering with punishment it seems the height of perversity to assert it can also be a privilege.

We can trace such a learning-experience in the sadistic story of Abraham and Isaac. Like most stories, it can be treated at many levels. At the *historical* level we re-enter the era when it was thought that a dangerous, angry god had to be appeased by the ultimate sacrifice of an Iphigenia or a Jephtha's daughter. In our own era we have been learning for ourselves that periodical blood-lettings – capital punishment, scapegoating, 'character assassination' – belong more to human sinfulness than to divine command.

At the *moral* level, where the story is primarily a test of faith and obedience, a sacrifice even greater than the ultimate sacrifice is being demanded. The pathos lies not merely in the killing of one's own flesh and blood; such an examination would be cruel enough. Abraham is asked in addition to forego all hopes of establishing a dynasty (through 'the only son'). Dreams of dynasty, immortality, vicarious success – all these are forms of tribalism from which parents have to be weaned at great cost, not least to their children.

A moral approach may take us so far: 'suffering is action and action suffering.' 'Whom he loves he chastens', perhaps. But such stoical sentiments leave us feeling like pawns on the cosmic chess-board:

> Like flies to wanton boys are we to the gods –
> They kill us for their sport.

As long as we are left dancing to the commands of a celestial puppeteer we resent our lot and kill 'Nobodaddy''. Whether resigned or resentful we are left feeling powerless actually to change the way things are. 'That's the way the cookie crumbles'; or, in more biblical terms, 'Man is born to trouble as sparks fly upwards' (Job 5, 7).

Every time, even with part of our minds, we subscribe to the notion that God needs to be appeased by some sacrificial (even self-sacrificial) gesture or offering, we have joined the puppets dancing on the strings. On this *theological* level we must firmly reject the model of a sadistic Father-figure requiring the death of his Son. All penal or sacrificial theories of the Atonement fall at the moral fence. If we accept that 'the Son of Man must suffer', it is as Representative Man, Ben-Adam, Everyman/woman, suffering for us but also with us and God in him, Emmanuel.

Moreover, there is a mysterious connexion between our experience and his: 'I in you and you in me'. Paul hints at it when he tells the Colossian Christians (1, 24): 'I fill up what is lacking (left over) in the afflictions of Christ in my flesh for his body's sake, the Church.' He shares ours as we share his. As the 2nd Century martyr Felicity cried before going into the arena 'Another suffers in me'.[16]

What defeats many people is making the connection between what happened to him then and what is happening to me, now. How do I convince the political prisoner held for months incommunicado, never knowing whether his tortures are being shared by his family or friends, that 'another suffers in you'? Writing to those Colossian Christians, Paul follows his enigmatic remark with a reference to their baptism. This is, he says, the way we become hands and feet of that battered body, die his death and live his life. Then, to illustrate the point, he introduces two inspired metaphors.

The first is the double 'nailing'. Let there be no doubt: we, the good people, 'the responsible society', put him there, doing the best we knew under the circumstances. That was our human attempt to lock God up – or out – to edge him out and put him where he no longer threatens us. But Paul sees another nailing: we nail up the evidence against us. Probably he knew of the label they pinned to the Cross as a kind of lampoon: 'King of the Jews'. That is what happens to self-styled 'liberators' – they come to a bad end. But Paul sees us nailing up the debt, the bill that is owing, our past record, from 'man's first disobedience and the fruit of that (other) forbidden tree . . . ' This bill, he says, has been paid; the estate agents have nailed up their sign-board to mark the completion of the deal. Sold, finished, consummatum est.

This introduces the second image – the triumphal procession which every victorious Roman general, like cup-winning athletes and football teams in our day, expected to stage as a public spectacle. 'Sing, my tongue, the glorious battle . . . ' On the day itself it feels like the end: only on the day after do we recognise it was only the end of the beginning. After VE and VJ Day the people recognised that the hard battles (smaller, less dramatic, but for many even more costly) lay ahead and not behind them. Bonhoeffer called this the 'hidden (or secret) discipleship'. It awaits the believer like the Spring but is hidden through the winter in the ground. The seeds of the real 'you', the Christ in you, are waiting to come fully alive. It only waits for Christ to speak his liberating word and bring us to life: new life 'hidden' in him.

THE SEED DIES

There are some sayings of Christ which come to us with the stamp of his total conviction and authority, prefaced by the solemn: 'Truly, truly I say to you . . . ' They seem to enunciate a universal truth with an immediate, personal reference. Such a saying introduces the Passion-Narrative in the Fourth Gospel. 'Si le grain ne meurt . . . ' Except the seed falls into the ground and dies, it stays alone. A truth certainly not unique to the Christian Gospel. The branches of the Golden Bough are laden with stories of dying and rising gods symbolising the death of nature in Winter and its coming to life again in Spring.

One such story, told by American Indians, refers to the discovery of corn. Every Spring, the eldest of the tribe goes into the forest to fast; he has to weaken and die if there is to be a good crop later in the year. One year, the elder had a vision of the god, Mondaumin, gaily decked in green and yellow, like our own Jack o' the Green or the Green Man. Challenged to fight, the elder succeeds in throwing him. He is told to bury his mysterious antagonist but to keep the grave free of weeds. Weeks later, two green shoots appear which turn brown, then golden. Today we can live on corn and do not have to kill for food. Si le grain ne meurt . . .

It is a biological fact that a seed comes to the point of death before it germinates; just as in child-birth the mother comes to the point of total exhaustion with all her strength spent before the child can be born. Christ takes this universal truth and applies it to his own story. The biological and universal are focussed in the particular and historical. Before the trap closes he has to explain why he has refused to evade it. He uses the visit of a small Greek delegation who approach him diffidently; but in this brief encounter he sees the harbinger of a cosmic future, the first wave of a mighty ocean. 'I, if I be lifted up, will draw all men to me.'

Moreover, he warns us that what is happening to him will happen to his followers also. Behind the hard sayings about 'denying ourselves', 'taking up our cross and following him', lies the observable truth that if you hug your security, cling to people or possessions and are not prepared to let go and allow the old to die, the new life cannot be born. If, like Silas Marner or old Mr Tulliver in 'Mill on the Floss', you hug your grumbles and grievances, you may become yourself a grumble or grievance: you may find yourself eaten up by your greed, anger, ambition or insecurity.

A TV Documentary brought this home to me. Four convicted rapists confronted four victims (not their own) in an American prison. Between them lay an unbridgeable chasm of total incomprehension. There was anger, grief, remorse, of course; but each side in the confrontation was locked up in a private prison where all were victims and there was no way out. Subsequently we were told that three of the rapists committed a similar crime after release.

A second group was filmed at Grendon, the psychiatric prison. All were convicted of violent crimes (murder, rape, armed robbery), but there was no confrontation between them and the psychiatric staff. Instead, there was evidence of a long process of reflection; each trying to get in touch with his feelings and his real self; finding that part of himself which must die if the true self was to be born. Too rare in the squalid, overcrowded conditions of our British prisons; but I have known one man, convicted of murdering his wife, going into prison smashed in little pieces, then emerging three years later, a whole person, grateful for the counselling of a Methodist Chaplain. 'He who hates his life in this world will find it for eternal life.' The seed that will not die, it is said, abides alone: no shoot, no harvest. Translated into international terms this points us to the necessarily painful process of sharing the world's resources spelt out in the Brandt and Palme Reports; in personal terms, it points us to the other painful process – being broken open, like the eucharistic loaf, so that we can find the neighbour and the Christ in him.

TRAGEDY & TRIUMPH

At the heart of Spring, in the events of Holy Week, the seed falls, dies and germinates. No other week in the year has such resonances of triumph and tragedy, with the focus shifting from public demonstration to private, domestic celebration; then back again to open confrontation, dénouement and execution.

> March is the month of morning,
>   Dews and dappled dawning,
>   No better to be born in.
> March the month of mourning;
>   A kiss beneath death's awning,
>   Crowds crowning and fools fawning –
> All blessed on Easter morning.

It is the time to stand up and be counted, whether marching to Aldermaston and Trafalgar Square or kneeling silently before an ominously hooded Cross. Of all the dramatic events, telescoped into a single week, the one portrayed by Leonardo da Vinci in his Last Supper that has entered almost every home, holds the still centre.

Many commentators are perplexed by the strange fact that the Fourth Gospel never actually records the institution of the Eucharist. John clearly sees the supper as a Passover meal. He gives us the image of the Good Shepherd who feeds the flock: the True Vine that gives life to the branches and enables them to 'bear fruit'; but no dominical command to 'do this in memory of me' such as we have in the other three Gospels and in the earliest account we have, in 1 Cor. 11, 23–26. Whether this is, as Temple implies,[17] because the celebration of the Eucharist was such a familiar part of every Christian's life and had already been fully recorded; or because John regarded the Feeding of the Multitude as itself a eucharistic meal – still, at this point there is an inexplicable hiatus and a resounding silence. The command 'Do This' is replaced by the New Commandment, and the institution of the Eucharist by the Master washing the feet of his friends. Perhaps in this dramatic acted parable he saw the key to the Friendship Meal as it has been enacted down the ages.

We have to set beside it the other scene on the previous night at Bethany. An unknown woman, widely thought of as Mary Magdalene or "Mary of Bethany", had washed his feet as he now washes his friends'. A simple, if costly, gesture accepted for what it is – a good deed. She has done the best she knows and followed her own truth. In performing this act of gratitude and devotion, both a menial service and a prophetic preparation for burial, she is also demonstrating (for all time, says Jesus,) the meaning of the New Commandment; like the whole Gospel, the two actions seen together overturn our commonly accepted ideas of Power and Love.

POWER & THE POWERLESS

The right use of power is the main issue of our day in Church and State alike. 'The collision of immoral power with powerless morality,' said Martin Luther King, 'constitutes the major crisis of our times . . . Properly understood, power is the ability to achieve purpose. At its best it is love implementing the demands of justice.'[18] We do well to treat it with caution and even suspicion: not to fight shy of it, remembering Hitler's famous dictum: 'Heaven is for sparrows and Christians – Earth is for us!' On the one hand, 'flower-power' may represent a retreat into a private world of fantasy and illusion: on the other, 'real power' may be equated with size, force or muscle-power. Whatever the sphere where it is exercised – economic or political, nuclear, union or woman-power – it cannot merely be tested by the clout it can wield; only by its 'ability to achieve purpose'.

On the way to Jerusalem the Twelve had been arguing about power and status: who should be Top People in the Kingdom? By putting a small child in the midst of them Jesus was giving a clear message that what really matters is to have the openness ('glasnost') and ability to grow and change that we associate with childhood. He charged them to have special care for the weak, vulnerable and (in the world's terms) powerless. 'The rulers of the gentiles are bosses . . . but it shall not be so amongst *you*.'

So now, at this crucial moment, he turns upside down our

ordinary notions of status and importance. He kneels down and washes their feet. Later on, at the trial before Pilate, the two images of power would confront each other, the two Kingdoms face to face. In that encounter the prisoner would say nothing in self-defence – such is the power of silence – but he, not the judge who delivers the sentence, is in command. Christ is silent before his accusers, says Origen, and leaves his whole defence in the lives of his followers.

In this one simple action, as in the whole Passion-story, there is a new kind of power at work: sacrificial, self-giving love. If his whole life was a Passion, a Book of Love (Liber Caritatis) laid out for all to read, it is summed up in this simple gesture which conveys the nature of love and the choices it presents. It is not primarily an emotional response (though this may have its own impetus); it is nearer to Gandhi's Satyagraha, acting out of love for truth. 'You see what I have done for you – you too must wash one another's feet.' Such power is inconsistent with absolute power, which 'corrupts absolutely', because it is delegated. Jesus confronts Pilate with the fact of dominion and, in the curious conversation about the nature of power, he shows where ultimate loyalty lies. 'The powers that be are ordained of God' – perhaps: but soon the early Christians would find themselves saying: 'We must obey God rather than men.' There is a clear line passing from Pilate's judgment-seat, through Luther ('Here I stand – I can do no other') and Bonhoeffer, to today's prisoners of conscience: all witnesses to the need to temper power with love and justice and always to subordinate it to the demands of truth.

'What is Truth?' asks Pilate, cynically. He is answered (if at all) by another question: the question-mark that overshadows the events of Good Friday and the enigma of Calvary. Why all this? Why does God allow it to happen? Why doesn't he intervene, do something . . . ? One of the most poignant pictures ever painted of the Passion is to be found in a Mediaeval Book of Hours, Les Heures de Rohan (1420–25). It depicts the dead Christ lying on the ground, just taken down from the Cross. John (or 'the Beloved Disciple') is supporting the Virgin, now his mother also, who is drooped over the body, holding out longing, lifeless hands to it. But John is looking back over his shoulder, glaring in agonised fury at God the Father whose hand is raised in blessing. He is confronting him with the unspoken question which any great tragedy leaves in the mind: Why?

The word is heard from the tortured lips of Jesus himself in the gathering, unnatural darkness: 'Eli, Eli, lama Sabachthani?' It is a terrible cry of protest and there is a note of distancing. No longer 'Father', but 'my God, my God'; it is the moment, says Harry Williams, when the idea of God as Father died on Jesus, the moment of separation and indescribable desolation. What can be said of no one else in history can be said of this lonely figure: he is God-forsaken.

We know, of course, that he was quoting Psalm 22. He was drawing on reserves of spirit as we all do in moments of acute distress. And this Psalm begins with a cry of protest when the poet, probably a Babylonian exile, is railing against the sufferings of his people. 'Why are we in this ghastly place?' He does not pretend to feel what he ought to feel – resignation, optimism, faith in God's providential care etc. He is angry and says so; like Job, Jonah and Jeremiah, he shakes his fist at God.

We know, too, that the poet works through his anger and frustration to a mood of 'hoping against hope' at the end of the poem. But for the moment all we have are the terrible opening words. They serve to remind us that Jesus is sharing the deepest, most intolerable pain of all, the darkness of depression. Anyone who thinks that the goal of human life is 'happiness' has to reckon with this cry. It shows up the vanity of human wishes, the superficiality of much that passes for happiness and may collapse like a pack of cards. Anyone who imagines that one just has to 'believe' for all the clouds to roll away has not reckoned with this cry. 'I wish I had your faith,' they say, as if 'faith' was an Aspirin or a Bandaid, some magical formula for removing pain!

In human experience 'joy and pain are woven fine' and the great questions: Why pain and evil? Why do the innocent suffer? Why do the wicked flourish as a green bay-tree? etc. continue to gnaw away at the back of the mind. As Von Hugel once said, 'Evil is a ghastly mystery and you don't get round it by calling it good.' And yet that cry on Calvary does give us some clues which may not provide any 'solution', but at least enable us to live with the

At the heart of the Eucharist is an empty Cross: and that Cross points us to the place of meeting between nature and grace, the horizontal and the vertical, when we know him in the breaking of the bread.

question. It reminds us, firstly, that there can be no true growth without conflict and real anguish, from birth to death. And no true humanity either. If life is a 'vale of soul-making', in Keats' phrase, this means *all* life, which includes our freedom to say No, to refuse love and to choose second best.

Secondly, Calvary shows us that the anguish of the world goes to the heart of God its Creator. If 'God was in Christ reconciling the world to himself, he was also in Christ protesting against the world, in Christ agonising on behalf of and in solidarity with the world. If Jesus was 'the human face of God' he was so still, even when that face was for a moment turned away from God or when his vision of God was obscured by self-doubt. If we believe that he was a window into the Love of God – 'He that has seen me has seen the Father' – he was so still, even when the window was clouded with pain. And perhaps never more so. For Calvary reminds us that God is never nearer to us than in our darkest and most desolate moments. He is infinitely vulnerable and, in the end, 'only a suffering God can help'.

But there is a final clue that comes from the Psalm that Jesus seems to have been reciting. As it unfolds, the poem moves from protest to a final resolution, a deeper faith and obedience. The question Why? may go on persistently nagging; but it is now put in a wider perspective, the ultimate purpose and providence of God. We only see this from hindsight, from the other side of the Passion, from the perspective of Easter and Resurrection. As a condemned prisoner once wrote on the walls of his cell, 'Par passage pénible, passons à port plaisant.'

But we do see it – and celebrate it – every time we rehearse or 're-present' the drama of the Passion at the Eucharist. It is then that the meaning of losing our selves in order to find our selves becomes plain: being broken open in order to be renewed and transformed. It is a daily or weekly re-enactment of the one saving event. And it is there that all those utterly human prayers: Give me, Thank You, I can't cope, and even Why me? Why all this? – all have their place. We pray them all in him and he in us. At the heart of the Eucharist is an empty Cross: and that Cross points us to the place of meeting between nature and grace, the horizontal and the vertical, when we know him in the breaking of the bread.

DARKNESS . . .

Between the darkness of Good Friday and the Easter dawn there is a pause. On this sabbath of sabbaths the battered body is at rest, as if the orchestra needed a rest before Agnus Dei can break into Alleluias. On this day, in Mediaeval England, 'the choirs would move through the churches carrying a piece of turf like a coffin, and all the while loudly bewailing the Lord's death.'[19] Just as their pagan ancestors had mourned the death of the Spring god; and as the Orthodox today retain the custom, carrying with great solemnity the epitaphion or recumbent crucifix, decked with flowers, out of the church for 'burial'. There has to be a 'real' death, with all the mourning and sense of loss, the darkness and vacuum of separation that we experience in bereavement. This death was (in Donne's word) 'ugsome' and the pain of it has to be drunk to the lees.

For many this provides the key that explains what is described symbolically as 'Descent into Hades', the place of waiting. Here again, the orthodox have captured the imagination with the icons that depict our Lord stepping down and extending a hand to Adam and Eve. The broken chains, the file, pincers and pliers lie around; and they are now free to move up into the realms of Easter light and the company of the redeemed. The one who could not be imprisoned in space is Lord of time and history: time itself is redeemed. Plato, Socrates and Aristotle have their honoured place in Greek frescoes of the Communion of Saints: they are now included under a canopy of Redemption that embraces all history and all time. Easter Eve symbolises the nadir of Incarnation, the neck of the hour-glass, when the world's fortunes began the long, slow, winding way up to fulfilment.

. . . BEFORE DAWN

As if to preserve our ancestral roots in the celebration of the dead and risen Adonis, the English have called their central festival of the year after the goddess of Spring, Eostre or Eastre (from the Greek Eos, Spring). Others believe the word derives from the old Teutonic 'urstan' (to rise) and 'urstand' (resurrection). There is something of a play upon words – or perhaps just a happy coincidence – that the Son's rising should be closely associated with Sun-rise: it is the day when the Sun/Son of Righteousness rose upon the darkness of the world with healing in his wings. If Christmas illumines 'the year's midnight' Easter lights up the early dawn. Whether it be Mary Magdalene groping her way through the garden to find the right tomb; or the Ethiopians on the roof of the Church of the Holy Sepulchre in Jerusalem, searching for the body they never find; or just little groups of friends fumbling for matches to light the Easter Fire as the vast orange of an African sun begins its slow ascent – this festival comes rosy-fingered in the Spring dawn. 'Eos', like 'Eros', must have its place in the scheme of things. At Easter it is as Dylan Thomas found it on Fern Hill

> . . . It was all
> Shining, it was Adam and maiden,
> The sky gathered again
> And the sun grew round that very day . . .

Some vital truth is lost if Easter is seen primarily as a past, historical event; or as the guarantee of a future – even an eternal future – that awaits us; and not primarily as a present experience and an undercurrent running through the whole of human life and through all creation. Nevertheless, scholars and theologians and, indeed, all who think it important to find 'a reason for the hope that is in us' must wrestle with the enigma of the Empty Tomb. By the very nature of things there could be no witnesses to the physical resurrection of Jesus: only to a disappearance and subsequent reappearance in a changed but instantly recognisable form. Accounts differ, but are congruous; we would be suspicious of a little fudging of the evidence if they agreed too closely. Anyway, too many were involved to make a proper, convincing conspiracy.

Each 'witness' recorded his or her special 'disclosure' in a manner which accorded with a particular personal need. Mary Magdalene had lost her closest friend and needed to know that he would now be even closer than before. Peter had lost his integrity and self-worth which could only be restored by an act of forgiveness, affirmation and total acceptance. Thomas needed to confront the limitations of critical intelligence and a failure of imagination compounded, perhaps, by his experience (as a twin) of mistaken identity. The friends at Emmaus, disenchanted by the failure of their national hero, needed to be reminded of the Suffering Servant: to have their eyes opened, to 'connect' and contextualise. Each disclosure was designed to meet each particular, personal need.

But these are not merely past events; they are also an intimate part of our contemporary experience. This is not to evade the mysterious and unique circumstances surrounding what has been described as the best-attested, as well as the most thoroughly researched and argued about, fact in history. Rather it is to look at the stories and ask the necessary question: 'What must have happened if those men and women described it in that way, their own different ways, and no other?'

Surely the best evidence for the truth of Easter lies where it has always lain, in the very existence of the Christian Church. A movement which should have petered out, as so many had before it, with the assassination of its leader, not merely survived but went on to proclaim to the world one truth only: that Jesus was alive, Christos Kyrios. But just as remarkable is the new perception of its two central symbols, the Eurcharist and the Cross. The meal which should have been a sad and solemn commemoration of a departed friend and teacher had become instead the means above all others of joyful reunion with a living Lord. The hideous gallows, the instrument of torture, ceased to be regarded as the supreme mark of degradation and became instead a symbol of life and forgiveness, a thing of beauty and a joy for ever: the signature marked on the forehead of every Christian to show he or she is 'Christ's person'. It will always remain in the end a futile, if perfectly natural, exercise to speculate what actually 'happened' on that first Easter morning. All we can usefully speak about are the effects of that 'happening', on the Church, the Eucharist and the Cross. It is not so much the empty tomb that requires the explanation, but rather the empty Cross.

> The tree of defeat became the tree of glory;
> And where life was lost, there life has been restored.

A NEW SPRING

How can this truth be released from its dogmatic chrysalis and become the means of transforming both our personal lives and the structures of our ailing institutions? Can it be the key to a restoration of our true relationship with the natural world; an end to our alienation and the birth of a new covenant with earth, its species and resources? This is the great debate of our times.

The pressures exerted on believers under regimes of left or right today do not arise out of their odd beliefs: it does not greatly worry anyone in any party caucus or government office if groups of people obstinately persist in believing in the Resurrection of the Body and the Life Everlasting. People hold far more exotic and eccentric beliefs than that and are relatively unmolested. What spells danger for those who deny human (or animal) rights is the belief that Christ is alive and can be encountered and recognised in every one of us: that the hairs of our head are all numbered, so that each individual and each creature has a unique value and destiny.

When Pope John Paul II visited Harlem he listened to the children singing and clapping. Then he said: 'If we are silent about the joy that comes from knowing Jesus the very stones in our cities would cry out. For we are an Easter people and Alleluia is our song.' A shiver of excitement ran through his audience as vivid and dangerous as an electric charge. They had come fully alive, not just half alive, content to 'go on living – living and partly living'. Perhaps it is only the Orthodox who have fully explored the mystery of Easter Death/Resurrection. The great Russian writers – Tolstoy, Dostoevsky, Solzhenitsyn, Pasternak – make it their recurrent theme. In Tolstoy's Resurrection, the hero faces his sentence, resolves to work out his regeneration and finds new life waiting for him in Siberia. Raskolnikov, the anti-hero of 'Crime and Punishment', is also condemned to Siberia. But he is raised to life again by his love for Sonia, the prostitute. He is made new. 'Life here,' says Dostoevsky, 'stepped into the place of theory, and something quite different would work itself out in his mind.'

Rabbi Lionel Blue has described how it felt to be a Jew visiting post-war Germany. He was anxious not to lose solidarity with his six million dead brothers and sisters, yet equally anxious to allow his German hosts to ask forgiveness without wallowing in guilt. The Jew in him had to die to allow the democratic fellow-human being in them to be born. Resurrection means coming to terms with your past, with history and tradition. Many liberation movements have not, and suffer from a lack of historical perspective. We have to be freed of our guilt for the past (slavery, industrial exploitation, colonial domination etc.): learn to live with the past and those bits of the past we would prefer to forget, and see them not as death-dealing 'guilt-trips', but as life-giving. The central importance of the Cross in Christian thinking lies in the transformation of an intrinsically evil situation into the source of the greatest good: the barrier has become a bridge. There is something to sing about after all.

NOTES

1. M.C. D'Arcy, 'Mind and Heart of Love', London, 1945, p. 64, where he makes a critique of the 'two loves hypothesis' and its principal exponent, Anders Nygren (in 'Agape and Eros').
2. James B. Nelson, 'Embodiment – an approach to sexuality and Christian Theology', London, 1979, p. 111. Ch. 5 gives a particularly helpful and balanced survey of a landscape which is something of a theological and ethical minefield.
3. Ibid. pp. 113–4.
4. Song of Songs 2, 11, where the beloved comes with the grace and agility of a young deer. It is as much a celebration of Spring as of love, human or divine. There could be no stronger argument for the inspiration of the compilers of the Canon than their decision to include this beautiful collection of Hebrew wedding-songs.
5. N. Berdyaev, 'Dream and Reality', London, 1950, p. 179: 'God has no power: he has less power than a policeman . . . God can reconcile man to the sufferings of creation because he himself suffers, not because he reigns. Pure monotheism is inconsistent with the Christian conception of God: in fact, it is the supreme form of idolatry.' Berdyaev developed a Philosophy of Freedom and was exercised with the question all his life. See also his 'Freedom and the Spirit' (1926).
6. Ibid. p. 46: 'Some have called me the philosopher of freedom . . . All my life I was engaged in hammering out a philosophy of freedom. I was moved by the basic conviction that God is truly present and operative only in freedom. Freedom alone should be recognised as possessing a sacred quality whilst all the other things to which a sacred character has been assigned by men since history began ought to be made null and void.' It was this conviction above all which made Berdyaev a life-long Socialist, but neither a Communist nor a practising Orthodox Christian.
7. Thomas Traherne (1637–74), 'Centuries of Meditation'.

8. John Burnaby, 'Amor Dei', London, 1938, p. 310. A fine exposition not merely of Augustine, but of the meaning of love. I am also greatly indebted to Charles Smyth, 'The Friendship of Christ' London, 1964.
9. Julian of Norwich (1373), 'Revelations of Divine Love', Ch. 5.
10. See 'Cry Justice' (ed. John de Gruchy), London, 1986, p. 126.
11. Neville Ward, 'Beyond Tomorrow', London, 1981, p. 99.
12. George Herbert, 'Lent', from The Temple (1633).
13. See Louis Fischer, 'Gandhi', Mentor, New York, 1954, pp. 75–6.
14. Jack Dominian, 'Cycles of Affirmation', London 1975, p. 161.
15. Hugh Montefiore, 'Jesus Across the Centuries', London 1983, see especially ch. 5, 'Jesus and the Abortive Coup'. He observes that uprisings were known to start in the desert; Josephus records such a revolt (Antiquities 20.8.6) and Paul was accused of leading a revolt of 4000 Assassins in the Wilderness (Acts 21, 38).
16. E.C.E. Owen, 'Some Authentic Acts of the Early Martyrs' (1927), pp. 74–92, for the story of Perpetua and Felicitas. Charles Williams in his 'Descent of the Dove' uses the saying to illustrate his 'doctrine of Exchange or Substituted Love'.
17. William Temple, 'Readings in St John's Gospel', London, 1945, p. 220.
18. Martin Luther King, 'Chaos or Community?', Penguin, 1969, p. 42.
19. L. Whistler, op. cit., p. 115.

4

High Summer

Existence is more than the taking of breath –
   There is more to the gift than the giving;
And dying is more than the moment of death,
   And life's more than a matter of living.

(Anon.)

. . . You have made an altar
out of the deck of the lost
trawler whose spars
are your cross . . .

(R.S. Thomas)

As the seasons change and Spring opens wings and windows to let in Summer, every day brings its own discovery of new strengths and possibilities. The adolescent/young adult wrestles with the agonies of identity-crisis: the question, 'Who am I?' inextricably bound up with the corresponding questions, 'What am I *for*? What am I meant to do with my life? Has God – if (s)he exists – a unique purpose for me? And do the qualities which I (think I) possess give any indication where and how that purpose is to be worked out?'

The movement into adulthood, away from the security of home and into uncharted waters and possibly unlooked-for responsibilities, brings its own growing-pains. In physics it is known as the loss of the Stable State, but it may (with reservations) be applied also to people and institutions.[1] It was experienced by the Church in the 5th Century as it watched the old world collapse with the sack of Rome and the fall of the Empire. Its protective framework of law and administration was replaced by a vastly inferior civilization. After the boisterous vigour of the first four Centuries the future looked grim and foreboding; some looked nostalgically backwards to what seemed like the green years of childhood and youth, rather as we do today to 'Edwardian summers'; others could only cling on and hope that the gates of Hell and vandalism would not prevail against the Rock of Ages.

We too may mourn the loss of the Stable State – not surprisingly after two centuries that have seen the greatest revolutions in our history, the Industrial and Computer Revolutions; when we are now faced with a world population of five billion and unprecedented threats to the continuance of life itself. Cavaliers ('wrong but Romantic') take refuge in nostalgia; Roundheads ('right but repulsive') dig in their heels and resist all change with stoical grit and determination; while some brave spirits welcome what they see as the creative action of a dynamic spirit and recall Newman's saying, 'to be human is to change; to be perfect is to have changed often.' Most of us, if we are honest, recognise variants of all three responses in ourselves. No one unreservedly welcomes change, while everyone accepts some change, even as a necessary evil. What feeds anxiety and angst is not so much change but the impact of ever-accelerating change such as Bonhoeffer in the 1940s, with his much-quoted 'mankind coming of age', could not have foreseen.

'AHA!' DISCLOSURES

Experience of radical change can bring what we may more properly describe in terms of revelation or resurrection. A relationship which we thought had gone dead suddenly bursts into flame; a seemingly intractable problem yields to a totally unlooked-for solution; after years of fruitless searching for a 'vocation', a life's work, the mists part and the way lies open and beyond all doubt. Jan Morris has described the moment of sex-change: whereas before, as James, she had felt at odds with herself and her gender, now for the first time she felt an integrated person. It was a moment of mystery, self-discovery and intense happiness.

'Resurrection is always a mystery', writes Harry Williams. 'It is always a miracle. It is always the creative act of the Eternal Word. Because that Word is spoken now in the present in terms of what we call the common circumstances of life, there can be nobody who at some time or other has not been thus raised from the dead. But more often than not our eyes are holden and we do not know it. We do not recognize resurrection when it comes to us. The presence of the Eternal Word is unnoticed, and evidenced only in the new life made available; just as at Cana of Galilee the guests enjoyed the good wine but did not know whence it was.'[2]

We may call these disclosures 'Aha!' moments, when our eyes are opened and we can only say: 'Of course! Why didn't I see it before?' . . . 'Then I was blind, now I can see.'

Such a moment awaited those two friends on the Easter road to Emmaus, a story which must rank with Joseph and his Brothers, the Homecoming of Odysseus and David and Jonathan as one of the most beautiful stories ever told. It has all the right ingredients: humanity, mystery, veracity. It portrays the human sadness and natural dejection of bereaved friends, transformed in a flash into unutterable joy. There is the patient unravelling of a problem: the stranger leads them gently through the history so that they can understand their own story as well as his. Jesus is the Rabbi right through; gentle and understanding, but firm with no pulled punches: 'O fools and slow of heart . . !' He that has eyes to see, let him see . . .

There is the mystery of hidden identity, the key to many great stories from 'Beauty and the Beast' to 'Twelfth Night' or 'Sleuth'. Who is the Stranger? We know, of course, but we have to go along with the incredible blindness of the two friends until the final dénouement. He says grace, breaks bread and – of course – it's Him! As in all good stories, there is a final scene; they have to do something, so they go off to share their experience with the Eleven and have their happiness confirmed.

We share the mystery and ask why they, like Mary Magdalene, were so blind. Was it a combination of grief, despair and sheer incomprehension? They were going through the valley of the shadow of bereavement and conscious only of their own loss, separation and abject disappointment – 'we'd trusted, and he's let us down.' They have to be released from the prison of preoccupation with themselves, their predicament and their dashed hopes, and focus instead on the object of their hope. The Stranger leads them through the events and shows the meaning and purpose behind them. It is the action of grace in showing us the way things are in an entirely new light. It does not remove the pain and grief: the events are still there, but they are experienced differently. The film has passed through the dark room and now the positives and negatives are reversed.

The Stranger shows them that there had to be a death. Being who he was and men being what they/we are, the Christ had to suffer. We know this in our minds – unless the seed falls into the ground and dies it cannot bear fruit. But when it happens we cannot bear it. We are overwhelmed by whatever it is – failure, sin, physical pain. We lose our bearings and need someone to show us the map and help us read the signs until our eyes are open and we can say: 'Of course! That's why I had to go through all that – how could I have missed the point?'

The real 'Aha!' moments are rare and unforgettable. They are surely the most rewarding features of a teacher's classroom experience. Who can forget the day when your child comes home and shouts in triumph for all the world to hear: 'I can READ, I can READ!' Then comes the moment when the full magic of Mozart casts its spell: or a picture makes its impact on the imagination. What had been quite familiar – perhaps too familiar – I see as if for the first time. The little Florentine has become Beatrice, the Vita Nuova and a glimpse of the Beatific Vision. This scaling away of a cataract from the mind's perception we may call Revelation or, with Harry Williams, Resurrection. It came to me quite unexpectedly one day in the Royal Academy, seated in front (or perhaps 'in the presence') of Cimabue's restored masterpeice of a Crucifixion, which itself experienced a kind of Resurrection.

RE-CREATION

On November 4th, 1966, the River Arno broke its banks and flooded the whole downtown area of the city of Florence. The devastation was greater than all the bombardment of World War 2. Of all the priceless treasures lost or damaged, the most important victim was Cimabue's Crucifix in the church of Santa Croce. When they waded through the sludge they found it had lost 60% of its painted surface. As they bore it off to the laboratory on an army lorry, boys sadly bowed their heads, the proudest and least religious of men interrupted their battle with the sludge and silently removed their hats. Many years later, after a most patient, skilful process of restoration, it was brought to the Academy in London, so that we, like those Florentine boys could silently bow our heads; but this time to welcome it 'dead but alive again, lost and found.' Ironically, what had been nearly destroyed by a so-called 'Act of God', man with his skills and devoted expertise had restored to a new and poignant beauty.

Then it was the whip
that flaked the flesh,
stripped and flailed to butcher's bone.

Now it is the flood
makes ruined majesty
of Cimabue's meditation;

Symbol of cruelty, redeemed by art,
unmade by cruel elements
and now remade by master-craftsmen.

Torn flesh, now flake by flake
restored, work perpetrated then
by man, now recreated,

You seemed always to wait
for Resurrection, as you bent
gently to one side to look on us.[3]

'There is always hope for a tree,' says Job gloomily in reply to Zophar – or, we may add, for a work of art. 'When felled it can start its life again; its shoots continue to sprout. Its roots may be decayed in the earth, its stump withering in the soil, but let it scent the water and it buds and puts out branches like a plant new set. But man? He dies, and lifeless he remains; man breathes his last and then where is he?' (14, 7–10) The water-course that had dried up in the great drought of 1976 would never, they said, recover – the water-table had sunk too low. This Spring it is a raging torrent, threatening to engulf the surrounding fields. Nothing in nature, even our excreta and waste products, is entirely lost; only recycled and served up in a new form tomorrow or the day after. Is it possible that we who are created 'a little lower than the angels' should find our ultimate destiny in providing a meal for worms and fishes? As some of our cancer patients put it: 'Death isn't the end, is it?' Is there a tomorrow beyond Donne's Good Morrow?

FEAR OF DEATH

Contemporary Christians are not conspicuously preoccupied with death or speculations about life after death. This may be because of the still lingering tabu and fear of 'morbidity' which surrounds it – it is commonly said that death is as much tabu for this generation as sex was for the Victorians; but, more positively, because we are more concerned with living the resurrection-life now, living God's Today which continues through death into his Tomorrow. The well-authenticated reports of those who have 'died' and been resuscitated may be interesting and even valuable; but Jesus' clear statement is enough for most of us, 'In my Father's house are many rooms . . .' (John 14, 2).

Nevertheless, each of us has to come to terms with death, our own and other people's. It may be that fear of death and what might follow in terms of 'punishment' or 'purgation' no longer haunts us as it did, for example, Dr. Johnson. If he wrote in the Vanity of Human Wishes of

> Faith that panting for a happier seat
> Counts death kind Nature's signal of retreat,

yet his prayers reflected a terror of death strange in such a devout believer. 'Death no man has escaped,' he said, 'and therefore no man can hope to escape it. From this dreadful expectation no shelter or refuge can be found. Whatever we see forces it upon us; whatever is, new or old, flourishing or declining, either directly or by very short deduction, leads man to the consideration of his end; and accordingly we find that the fear of death has always been considered as the great enemy of human quiet, the polluter of the feast of happiness, and embitterer of the cup of joy.'[4] John Donne spent many nights lying in his coffin and had himself depicted in his shroud to help him 'memento mori'. But in our day advances in anaesthetics have removed much of the anguish of dying. As with the perils of child-birth, death is no longer a near and dreaded neighbour – more of a distant friend.

Moreover, increased longevity and our confident expectation to exceed the Psalmist's span of three-score years and ten has changed our attitude to death. As Jacques Pohier argues in his 'God in Fragments', 'we are the first human beings to be able to note empirically that death is not a setback to life, an accident coming to life from outside it, but is part of life, natural to life, a stage of life which is not contrary to it nor its enemy.' Our concern, therefore, should not be artificially to prolong life, but to enrich it as long as it still has value and quality and has not become simply a burden. 'It is no longer a matter,' he says, 'as it was for millennia, of adding years to life; it is a matter of adding life to years.'[5] Rightly understood, life and death should be seen not in opposition but in partnership, like the horses held together in harness by Plato's charioteer: the two wheels of the bicycle that ensure its progress. Without a full stop this manuscript would either continue interminably (which is unthinkable!) or could not continue at all.

Nevertheless, coming to terms with premature, sudden or accidental death or the death of a young and promising adult with all the world before him/her, is another matter. Many would agree with Sir Geoffrey Jackson, the Ambassador, who was taken hostage and held for months in solitary confinement and in daily expectation of execution, when he said he had come to terms with his own death, but certainly not with his wife's. We have all at some time woken up in tears after a bad dream in which some beloved member of the family had died: a remote preparation, perhaps, for the inevitable experience of bereavement. This preparation begins in childhood with the death of pets and animals when we learn not that 'God has taken them', but that 'God is caring for them – underneath are the everlasting arms.' We learn something about death with physical separation; every parting is a small death. Every night we entrust our spirit into the hands of God, as the lovely Compline prayer points us to him who at the evening hour 'didst rest in the sepulchre, and didst thereby sanctify the grave to be a bed of hope to thy people.'

Jesus was most careful to prepare his friends for their coming bereavement. Not only in the Farewell Discourse of John 14–17, but in the three-fold predictions of his Passion (e.g. Mark 8, 31; 9, 31; 10, 33–34). The warnings were clearly not understood at the time; but they were remembered, recorded and recalled by the early Christians to substantiate their claim that 'it was ordained that the Christ should suffer and so enter into his glory' (Luke 24, 26).

The death and raising of Lazarus (who may possibly be disguised as 'the Beloved Disciple') represents a stage in the learning process and a preparation for Jesus' own Death and Resurrection.

The question posed by the two Bethany sisters in turn: 'Why did you let this happen – to him, to us?' is the question uppermost in the minds of the bereaved. Why did you let him – of all people – slip away from us? He could have prevented it; of that the sisters are sure. But he deliberately delayed – why? Jesus responds by questioning their understanding of death and resurrection. He begins where they are and with the hope that was generally shared – 'this life can't be all there is; there must be something *more*.' He then leads them on to think of life before death, the life that continues through death, which he brings for us to share 'in him'. Naturally, this could only be intelligible in the light of Easter and his own Resurrection, enabling Paul to ask: 'Were you not raised to life with Christ?' But for the moment it was enough that they should acknowledge some radically new experience, foreshadowed by the raising of Lazarus and symbolized for us in the death-resurrection event of Baptism: 'you have already died and your life is hid with Christ in God' – you have already risen and are already living the resurrection-life.

Jesus uses the experience of bereavement, a family tragedy which he shares to the full, as a learning-experience, an occasion for growth, the gaining of new vision and a deeper grasp of truth. 'I am glad for your sakes I wasn't here.' Even this, the greatest imaginable disaster, is an occasion for gratitude: 'Father, I thank you . . . ' It dominates everything else – his natural grief and sense of loss, his awareness of surrounding danger, his solidarity with a family that has provided him with the nearest approximation to a home. Those words with which we greet and say farewell to 'the faithful departed' are an affirmation of God's yes to human life that needs death for its continuance. And if, as Tillich says, 'joy is the emotional expression of the courageous yes to one's true being', it is an occasion of thanksgiving when we can say without fatalism or false optimism with St Francis: 'Welcome, Sister Death!'

Where fear remains, it is rather fear of cosmic annihilation, because we do not have to be reminded that we live and have lived for the past forty years under a Balance of Terror, within four to seven minutes of extinction. It is an intolerable thought and most of us delegate to others the task of thinking the unthinkable – to experts, think-tanks or moral theologians who can make nice distinctions between just and unjust wars. The very thought even of surviving nuclear catastrophe, in the grey half-light of a nuclear winter, induces feelings of physical nausea; or, what is more insidious and more difficult to assess, encourages cynicism, fatalism or despair. It may be that images of nuclear holocaust have largely supplanted those other images of the Last Judgment and the great Doom-paintings familiar to our ancestors: the terrifying sermons on the pains of the damned which James Joyce, in his 'Portrait of the Artist as a Young Man', recalls from the days of his Jesuit education. Ours is a different nightmare, and the conscious mind develops its own resistances to it.

DYING WELL

Many who have successfully come to terms with the inevitability of death – their own or their partner's – have not come to terms with the actual process of dying. It may well be that 'change and decay in all around we see', but still we secretly dread the whole process: decline, diminishment, disintegration, failing powers, increased dependence on others, while we wait at the 'terminus' for the train that never seems to arrive. Society reacts by locking away the senile; by institutionalising the elderly and delegating their care to dedicated professionals, we make life more tolerable for ourselves, if not always for our patients. It is only when the skill of those who 'strive officiously to keep alive' has added significantly to the numbers involved that we turn once more to 'community care' and ask families to resume responsibilities which in less developed societies they have always accepted. There is no decision more difficult to take or more fraught with feelings of guilt and divided loyalty than that of delegating to others the care of the elderly. And it is usually women – and chiefly the unmarried daughters – on whom the burden of caring is bound to fall.

It is made easier by the growth of the Hospice Movement. Rather than allow people to die in hospitals, where death is inevitably seen in terms of defeat and failure, access to hospice care (including the services of nurses with proper pain-killing facilities) has enabled many to approach death, not merely with dignity, but surrounded by all the familiar faces and associations that bring comfort and reassurance for the final journey. If we judge the quality of life in our society by the quality of care extended to those who have a slender grasp of it, we should ensure that hospice care is available to all who wish it and not, as at present, only to the fortunate minority. While it remains a relative 'luxury', hospitals will continue to provide services for the dying which they are, by their very nature, unable to fulfil. Death will be seen either as a defeat or as an unmitigated evil to be postponed by transplants and ever more sophisticated means of artificially prolonging life; we shall simply be 'adding years to life' without significantly 'adding life to years'.

To celebrate Easter is to acknowledge that life is stronger than death: that however inevitable (and Shaw's 'Back to Methuselah' may remind us quite how boring life would become without it), even painful and distressing for those who are left behind, it does not have the last word. Death is only an evil or an 'enemy' if it is not counted as 'a bed of hope to God's people'; if it is seen as the final curtain coming down at the end of the Play, and not as the curtain going up on Act I, at the end of a long and often tedious Dress Rehearsal. Part, at least, of this 'rehearsing' must include coming to terms with the whole process of dying and rising, losing and finding, holding on and letting go, giving and receiving back, which is both my experience of finitude and creaturehood and also my intimation of an eternal destiny as part of the New Creation.

Easter demonstrates in symbolical, liturgical form the essential truth that life and death are not separate, consecutive events. They may come serially but they belong together. Both are now. Dying we live and living we 'die daily' and learn a little more each day to die well. This may be a painful but it is in no sense a gloomy truth. I once attended, together with doctors, nurses and members of the 'caring professions' a workshop on death, dying and bereavement. In the course of it we discovered that we each had pieces of unfinished business with the dead – parents, grandparents, ancestors – to complete. One member needed to make peace with three unborn, aborted babies. We shared unresolved guilt-feelings, our regrets about unspoken love, suppressed anger. As the week-end unfolded, we were enabled to agonise but also to laugh a little together. But we recognised that as long as we kept the fact of death at arm's length we should be unable to meet it in or with others.

One exercise was to say, in role-play, to another: 'I am your death and your friend. What do you wish to tell me or hear from me?' Most of us are more than ready to hear the truth, however negative the prognosis; the truth sets us free to give ourselves fully to the time that remains. Some simply do not want to know – or not yet. But at whatever level is tolerable, the truth as far as it is known (and it is never definitive) must be conveyed not brutally but sensitively, compassionately, from someone who will stay with us and help us absorb it at our own pace. At hospices and in nursing-homes, like the Marie Curie Home where I was privileged to work, staff may sit for hours with patients, winning their confidence and sharing their natural fears and apprehension. It is never justifiable, even with the highest motives and the best intentions, to foist our own beliefs in Resurrection or Life After Death on patients who may not have given much thought to such questions before the onset of terminal illness.

Those who have a mature conviction that 'all shall be well and all manner of thing shall be well' have by and large made their own preparation for the journey. They will be gathered to their fathers (or mothers): be absorbed into Nirvana: go home to God – in whatever terms their faith defines. Those who are convinced that this life is all there is – the candle is snuffed, the curtain falls and the play is ended – these have made their own adjustment. Those who need friendship, encouragement and reassurance are the ones who are not sure and for whom death is a nagging question-mark: 'Death isn't the *end*, is it?' 'Surely there must be something *more*?' Even convinced and practising Christians can be muddled and confused: not all who believe in God necessarily hope for life continuing through death; strangely enough, some are quite convinced there is life after death but have no belief in God. What can be helpful is to allow the patient to articulate such beliefs as are held, to tell his own story in his own terms.

One of our own patients in the Home, a New Zealander, was a boat-builder by profession. He arrived bringing armfuls of plans and drawings, designs for the most beautiful boat he had ever built, on which he intended to sail round the world. We all enjoyed poring over the plans, sharing his enthusiasm. We even found a warehouse on the Thames where it might be built. As the months wore on, the patient grew weaker and it became plain to him, as it had been to us for some time, that the boat would never be built.

But he never put away the designs and continued to make adjustments and refinements to them. For the boat he was building was his 'Ship of Death' on which he was to embark and voyage into uncharted waters. Designing it was his way of preparing for death: that was the way he was telling his story in the terms he knew best. It would not only have been callous but also, in the deepest sense, untrue if we had told him that the boat would never be completed or needed. He embarked on it when he was ready, and our part was to be the warehouse and the wharf: to share his story and enable him to live it to the full until God called him home.

LIFE AFTER LIFE

This is not to say that what we believe about life after death is of no consequence; nor that our beliefs about death itself will not affect the way we approach it. Certainly, convinced believers do not always 'make a good death'. Isaac Watts knew all about the 'gloomy doubts' that prevent us seeing 'the Canaan that we love with unbeclouded eyes':

> But timorous mortals start and shrink
> To cross the narrow sea,
> And linger shivering on the brink
> And fear to launch away.

Firm belief does not always confer courage; nor does orthodoxy convey a future life insurance policy or rescue us from the vale of tears. Parting, bereavement, physical separation are as painful for the believer as for the unbeliever, for though the prospect of reunion may soften the blow, the wound remains. Physical death stands as a telos, a terminus, even when we remember that the terminus is a place for changing trains and continuing our journey.

The real value of a belief in the Resurrection of the Body lies not in our approach to life after death but in the way we approach life before death. If we believe with Paul that 'the spirit of him who raised Jesus from the dead . . . will give life to your own mortal bodies through his Spirit living in you', that will affect the value we place on the life of the senses, aesthetic joys and experience, institutions, the bricks and mortar of daily life. Things of beauty can indeed be seen as 'joys for ever' and the life of the imagination take on eternal significance. As in Ezekiel's great vision, God can make of these 'dry bones' a living, Spirit-filled means of grace and hope of glory. To believe that this life 'is all there is' does not place greater value upon it, as Marxists would have us suppose, but subtly devalues it. And to believe in the Resurrection of the Body, its sensuality, sexuality and infinite capacity for change and renewal, is to give it the exalted status conferred by Paul when he called it the Temple of the Spirit. 'Eye has not seen nor ear heard . . . what God has prepared for those who love him' (1 Cor. 2, 9).

If we look for evidence we may be encouraged by the numerous stories of survival such as those recounted by Dr. Raymond Moody. The patients he worked with spoke of 'out of the body' experiences, reunion with departed relatives and friends, an approach to 'some sort of barrier or border, apparently representing the limit between earthly life and the next life'; then return, with intense feelings of joy, love and peace and reunion with the physical body. Dr. Elizabeth Kubler-Ross, author of the classic 'On Death and Dying', confirms that this coincides with her own researches, that 'the dying patient continues to have a conscious awareness of his environment after being pronounced clinically dead.'

'All of these patients,' she writes, 'have experienced a floating out of their physical bodies, associated with a great sense of peace and wholeness. Most were aware of another person who helped them in their transition to another plane of existence. Most were greeted by loved ones who had died before them, or by a religious figure who was significant in their life and who coincided, naturally, with their own religious beliefs.'[6]

Nevertheless, it must be firmly stated that 'resuscitation', like that of Lazarus, is not 'resurrection'. After-death experiences only confirm that the frontier between life and death is more blurred than we have been led to imagine; and their principal value for us is that they remove some of the fears and anxieties that cloud our progress into 'the undiscovered country from whose bourn no traveller returns'. Kubler-Ross has stated unequivocally that 'none of the patients who have had a death-experience – and returned – is ever afraid to die.'

Moreover, these experiences are more of separation of soul/

psyche/personality from the body than of their reunion, completion and reintegration. Belief in immortality, the survival of the psyche, may mean (as the Greeks saw it) the shedding of the encumbrances of the material world – the soma/sema, body/tomb. The body is seen as a kind of envelope which can be thrown away when the letter, conveying the essential 'message', has been delivered. Survival may mean simply that (as C.D. Broad thought) 'certain people survive death for a certain period of time'. This seems to have been J.B. Priestley's view when, in his play 'Johnson Over Jordan', historical characters continue to live and thrive as long as they are remembered, but their 'vigour' depends on the willingness of future generations to keep that memory fresh and honoured.

Christian confidence in Resurrection, on the other hand, can only be soundly based on the attested fact of Jesus' Resurrection and what those accounts tell us of his identity with and transformation of the Jesus they had known before. He seems to have been instantly recognisable to some (e.g. the disciples in the Upper Room) but not to others (e.g. Mary Magdalene and the friends at Emmaus). His body was identical with the body that had died, bearing the stigmata; he could eat breakfast and converse as before. But he was free of all spacio-temporal limitations. This blend of identity and transformation is taken by Paul as the paradigm for our own resurrection: 'You sow a bare grain, say of wheat, and then God gives it the sort of body that he has chosen; each sort of seed gets its own sort of body' (1 Cor. 15, 37–38).

Beyond the evidence of the Gospels we can only appeal to the evidence of the natural world, the cycle of seasons and our own experience of dying and rising, being lost and found, 'belonging hopelessly to the past and our being raised up to the creative call of our own future.'[7] It remains a grace, a given: our recreation as miraculous as our original creation. 'For Resurrection is God creating,' says Williams, 'and that passes infinitely beyond the range of our conceptual or linguistic machinery. If we think we have successfully nailed resurrection to the wall, then we are worshipping an idol, and when it is shown up for what it is we shall feel the need to rush to its defence.' Meanwhile, we are left with symbols, images, intimations that point to a reality and fulfilment we can only hope and prepare for. 'We die but to be reborn. And exactly how we go through the last door, how we die, will depend on how we respond to the many hourly, daily, yearly experiences of dying that we encounter in our lives; how we respond to the dying of a dream, a friendship, an ambition, a passion.'[8]

THE GREEN & THE RED

As Eastertide draws to its close, two Festivals prepare us for the coming of Summer: St George's Day and May Day. True, St George has been demoted in the Calendar largely because of the paucity of historical data; his significance has always been more symbolical than historical/theological. Like Marduk in Egyptian or Perseus in Greek mythology – both distinguished dragon-slayers – he has represented for generations the triumph of good over evil forces, symbolised by the unfortunate dragon. As such he has been adopted as their patron saint by people as widely different as Greeks, Ethiopians and Portuguese: the returning Crusaders attributed their victory at Antioch in 1098 to the Saint's direct intervention (like that of the Angel of Mons) which encouraged the English to adopt him as their patron also. He was the ideal soldier-hero – the officer in the Roman army martyred for his faith under Diocletian – around whom other legends gathered. In addition to the standard story of the rescue of the princess from the power of the dragon there is a Coptic legend which tells of St George's body being cut to pieces, scattered throughout the land, then reassembled by the Archangel Michael and brought back to life by God.

This clear association with Resurrection is underlined by his banner, the red cross on the white ground, which mediaeval artists gave the Risen Christ. But it is more probably his association with Spring than with Easter that has occasioned his widespread popularity. The dragon he defeated was the symbol of darkness and chaos; he comes to assure us that Spring is really here. His very name 'Georgos' (in Greek, a tiller of earth) makes him more a fertility than a macho-military figure, He is the Green Knight celebrated by the hobby-horse mock joustings at Padstow in Cornwall where they sing:

> Awake St George our English Knight O
> For summer is acome O and winter is ago,
> And every day God gives us grace
> By day and by night O.[9]

It is reassuring to find that one whom we have always thought to be a symbol of nationalism and militarism is really a farmer: he is Green George after all! He may have been a Roman soldier and the dragon may have been a crocodile. The fact that Uccello's George is piercing its eye and not its throat may be the artist's way of showing that he knows this to be the vulnerable part of the crocodile's anatomy. But he is also Marduk, the Babylonian storm-god, cutting the monster Tiamat in two and holding apart the earth from the floods above and beneath; he is Perseus and Hercules, Launcelot and Mister Valiant-for-Truth. We need our heroes, but not to bolster the little tin gods of jingoism and nationalism. And no better hero than Shakespeare, who was born and reputedly also died on St George's Day. His festival at Stratford-on-Avon is bedecked with the flags of every nationality; like St George, he belongs not just to England but to the world. Both are legitimate causes and stimulants of national pride, but they have little to do with the vulgar and destructive nationalism which has brought misery to millions of its victims.

For true internationalism we must look to May Day with its processions and banners which proclaim: 'Workers of the World Unite!' Traditional may-poles still survive; flower-festivals like the Derbyshire well-dressings still remind us of links with the celebration of the festival of Flora, the goddess of flowers, in Roman Britain. There is about these festivals a touch of melancholy, as if the very fleetingness and fragility of the garlands and flower-mosaics were reminding us of the tragic transience of natural beauty and the corruptibility of even the finest products of the natural order. The grass withers, the flower fades . . . or, as the Mayers' song goes:

Remember us poor Mayers all
  And thus do we begin
To lead our lives in righteousness
  Or else we die in sin . . .

. . . The life of man is but a span,
  It flourishes like a flower.
We are here today and gone tomorrow
  And we are dead in an hour.

A thing of beauty is not necessarily a joy for ever. Keats was a victim of the romantic illusion that 'Beauty is Truth, Truth Beauty: that is all ye know on earth and all you need to know.' A flower is a symbol of human mortality and finitude because it is demonstrably untrue that 'its loveliness increases, it will never/Pass into nothingness'. It may be a bulwark against barbarism and philistinism and prevent us thinking that the mind is all, economics is all, even that 'love is all'. But if we imagine that beauty is all we have fallen victims of the 20th Century disease of nostalgia; it has become an idol, a distraction from the innerness of truth, Hopkins' 'inscape'. When Jesus told us to learn (katamathete) from the lilies of the field, he was telling us to open our eyes to the mysteries of growth and the flower's dependence on the grower. Heaven and earth shall pass away; only Truth abides for ever.

May Day celebrations have seldom been closely associated with the Church – which may partly explain why it was chosen for Labour Day! May for Catholics is Mary's Month, which makes Hopkins ask: 'Why fasten up on her, with a feasting in her honour?' and reply:

> All things rising, all things sizing
> Mary sees, sympathising
> With that world of good,
> Nature's motherhood.

But if the month belongs to Mary, the day itself belongs to Philip and James; linked together, like Peter and Paul or Simon and Jude, perhaps to denote the sending out of the Apostles in pairs. The Gospel for the day (John 14, 1–14) contains not only the saying which gives it its theme: 'I am the Way, the Truth and the Life', but also the promise which points us directly to Rogationtide; 'If you ask anything in my name, I will do it.'

PEACE WITH EARTH

The old custom of 'beating the bounds' of the parish at Rogationtide has fallen into disuse and merits revival in an age when none of us can opt out of concern with the environment and ecological issues. It sprang from the year 465 A.D. and the terrible earthquake in S. France, when Mamertus, Bishop of Vienne, near Lyons, ordered that his congregations should process round the ruined fields and pray for God's blessing on the crops. He was probably drawing on an earlier custom of beating the bounds, taken in its turn from the festivals of Terminalia and Ambarvalia in the Roman world. Crowds would move around the corn-fields, with singing and dancing, driving away winter with their sticks and sacrifices.[10]

Hence, an annual 'Perambulation of the Circuits of Parishes' became a special feature of Rogationtide. The Litany, with Psalms 103 and 104, would be recited on the way at different stations. The Elizabethan Injunctions of 1559 refer to sacred and secular purposes; they were to ask God's blessing on the land and its fruits, but also to 'consider the old ancient bounds and limits belonging to our township' – in short, be aware of the neighbourhood. One of the local boys would even be 'bumped' against the boundary-stones or ducked in the pond to ensure that successive generations should have an active memory of the site if ever disputes over boundaries should arise. This may explain why in the Laws of King Alfred and Athelstan Rogation days were called not only 'gebeddoegas' (Prayer Days) but also 'gang doegas' (Gang Days), as in parts of the North of England they still are. Bishop Cosin of Durham has left us a fine prayer for the environment:

> Almighty God, Lord of Heaven and Earth, in Whom we live and move and have our being; Who dost good unto all men, making Thy sun to rise on the evil and the good, and sending rain on the just and on the unjust; favourably behold us Thy people, who call upon Thy Name, and send us Thy Blessing from heaven in giving us fruitful seasons, and filling our hearts with food and gladness; that both our hearts and mouths may be continually filled with Thy praises, giving thanks to Thee in Thy Holy Church through Jesus Christ our Lord.[11]

Rogationtide has sometimes been decried and ridiculed as a futile and pre-scientific exercise of praying for fine weather. A better response, it is said, to the vagaries of our climate would be to build a silo. But in an age when we are creating deserts and dust-bowls at an unprecedented rate: when the great rain-forests of Panama and

South America that have taken forty million years to grow, with all their teeming species and abundance of wildlife, are being razed to the ground in half an hour, it is already five minutes to midnight. Shall we continue our feverish preoccupation with quick profits in the short-term, or focus on the Kingdom of Earth and our relationship with it? 'The more you believe in the Incarnation,' said Henry Scott Holland, 'the more you care about drains.' The more we work for peace *on* earth, the more closely should we be concerned for our peace *with* earth.

'Beating the bounds' reminds us that there are necessary limits within which we work: parishes, described by Coleridge as 'God's unobtrusive, continuous agency', which are neither the whole Kingdom of God nor little fiefdoms where clerical domination holds undisputed sway; but small mustard-seeds from which the Kingdom grows. Eternity is still (in Blake's phrase) 'in love with the productions of time' and there have to be times and places where 'rich and poor in countless lands reach out their hands to take God's holy food'. To ignore boundaries, limits and markers is to risk falling victims of 'anomie' and to forget that they provide opportunities for creativity and growth. Order and organisation, systems and institutions are necessary (even a necessary evil, perhaps) if individuals are to be enabled to make their own unique contribution. 'Don't mourn, organise!' was the cry of 19th Century trade unionists who saw clearly that collective action, which demands visibly defined cooperation and coordination, is the only adequate response to social evils.

Nevertheless, boundaries can become oppressive if the 'system' becomes an end in itself; they can induce a blinkered parochialism and blind us to the wider vision of a Wesley for whom the world was his parish. Justice and mercy begin at home, where we are; but, like the source of a river they can become a mere swamp if they stay there and do not flow where the slant of God's Spirit carries them. Virginia Woolf's reminder that 'the Nile flows through our living-rooms' echoes some words of Augustine:

> You are the Body of Christ, that is to say, in you and through you the method and work of the Incarnation must go forward. You are meant to incarnate in your lives the theme of your adoration. You are to be taken, consecrated, broken and

distributed that you may be the means of grace and vehicles of Eternal Charity.'[12]

NEW PERSPECTIVES

If Rogationtide draws our attention to the environment and the horizontal dimension, Ascensiontide lifts our eyes up and makes us aware of the vertical and transcendent. Immersed in the insatiable demands of the present moment, we may lapse into cynicism or despair; the issues are mostly complex, very few are clear-cut, and our energies are easily dissipated in mere activity. The system, the organization, makes total demands that we cannot honestly meet. Alternatively, we become slaves of fashion and follow any 'ism' or 'wasm' currently on offer. To be open to the future while giving full value to the claims of the present, the neighbour who confronts me, requires a constant adjustment of perspective. 'We cannot be swallowed up by the present age because we are bound to the future and because we experience the future in the present.' Leech, who quotes those words of the German theologian, Christoph Blumhardt, comments: 'It is the God who is always beyond us, always future, always moving onwards, who prevents us from being enslaved to passing trends and to the present age.'[13]

Such is our hunger for the transcendent and the extra-terrestrial dimension that an event like the Ascension of Christ seems to point to the world of Star Wars, Sci-Fi and Close Encounters of the Third Kind. Spielberg has been highly successful in tapping primal instincts within the human psyche, peering into that god-shaped hole in us. Perhaps that explains the popularity of a genre exploited to the full by C.S. Lewis in his 'Narnia' novels, which casts a spell of the 'mysterium tremendum et fascinans' over young and old alike. Children are fascinated, not frightened like the adults, and find their attention riveted to the conflict or cooperation between earthlings and visitors from outer space. We have to be brought back to earth by the rebuke of those other 'extra-terrestrials': 'Ye men of Galilee, why stand ye gazing *up*?'

There are undeniably bad reasons for 'gazing up'. Escaping into a world where homelessness, famine and unemployment do not happen: nostalgia for the days that are no more – those friens meeting on the hill must still have been working through their grief, exchanging memories of the Master who had come back to them in ways surpassing their wildest dreams, but would not come back in the same way again. They had to be given an opportunity to say goodbye before they could give themselves to the task assigned to just eleven bereaved and rather bewildered men: no less than 'making disciples of all nations', the regeneration of all mankind! One chapter had to be closed before the great new chapter could begin; as with our own lesser bereavements, some 'rite de passage' had to be undergone to mark the end of the old physical, tangible relationship.

Instead of 'Ascension' it would be better to speak of 'withdrawal' or 'departure', as Luke's word 'dieste' (he was parted from them) denotes. In his second account (Acts 1, 2), the word 'anelephthe' could as easily be translated 'taken *away*' as 'taken *up*'. And while the language of clouds, space and removal naturally pointed upwards (so that some Mediaeval painters depicting the event had to mark this by the two feet sticking through the bottom of a cloud), there is no evidence that the Evangelists would have been deceived by spacial metaphors. Physical withdrawal was necessary if Jesus was to be universally acknowledged. 'He has gone into all the world, lady,' says Masefield's Pilate to his wife. The Jewish Rabbi who had under the conditions and restraints of Incarnation, belonged to a particular time, place and culture was henceforth omnipresent, 'the same yesterday, today and for ever', and his authority universal. What they experienced as loss and bereavement we know to have been liberation.[14]

So there are also good reasons for 'gazing up', lifting our eyes to the hills . . . I am enabled to see my true potential: direct my attention at the goal of my journey and see what can be done and remains to be done. This is not to indulge in romantic day-dreams and Utopian fantasies. Wilberforce in his day was dismissed as a dangerous fanatic whose dream of an end to the slave-trade made no economic sense (by hindsight we see that it did) and for some spelt commercial ruin. Those who work to end the arms-trade today and even dream of a nuclear-free world – or at least a world relieved of the shadow of nuclear weapons – are similarly dismissed as Utopian. But to have your sights raised is to be given the courage to dream; Wilberforce took thirty-five years to make his dream a reality.

To raise your sights is to become dissatisfied with what is: the first step to moving on to what might be/can become. It denotes a mood of expectancy; not waiting for something to turn up in Micawberish fashion, but certainly waiting. Waiting, as the Eleven were told to wait, for 'empowerment' means being open to the utterly unexpected, to what we secretly dread quite as much as what we more confidently expect. People can expect too little, for fear of disappointment; or too much, which makes that disappointment inevitable; or nothing at all, which means that we continue to travel without any real hope of arrival. The only promise we were assured of was: 'Fear not, little flock, it is the Father's good pleasure to give you the Kingdom.' That, and the final promise: 'I shall be with you till the end of the Age.' How that promise was kept is the story of Whitsun.

THE ELEMENTAL DANCE

Although it is the third of the great Trinity of Festivals that mark the high-points of the Christian year, it has never captured popular imagination and affection to any degree comparable with Christmas and Easter. Even its name is confusing. The original name, Pentecost, ties it to its Jewish roots, being the fiftieth day after the Passover Sabbath; it commemorated the giving of the Law to Moses when Israel was designated 'a peculiar treasure, a kingdom of priests and a holy nation' (Exod. 19, 5, 6). No doubt this event, reaffirming their Abrahamic election, was foremost in the minds of those devout Jews of the Diaspora gathered in Jerusalem to celebrate their Pentecost. But now they were to witness the establishment of a New Israel, 'a royal priesthood, an holy nation, a peculiar people' (1 Peter 2, 9) which would not easily accommodate itself to the old.

The English name bears its own ambiguity. 'White' arose most probably from the white robes of the newly baptised (the word is derived from the Saxon 'Hwita Sunnandaeg'); but our ancestors also spelt it 'Wit', reminding us of the gift of wisdom or 'right judgement in all things' which the Spirit confers:

> Come Lord, come wisdom, love and power . . .

> Enable with perpetual light
> The dullness of our blinded sight.

There is also an ambiguity in its liturgical colour which is not white (as for Christmas and Easter), but flaming, fiery red, the colour of the cloven tongues. Whit walks may bring out the children to process in immaculate white shirts and dresses through our Northern towns; Whit weddings may retain their popularity, all decked out in that optimistically unadulterated white. But at its heart Pentecost speaks not so much of the whiteness of new birth as of the warmth of new fire. The images it evokes are those of power: the elemental forces of water, wind and fire. Whereas Christmas celebrates the light shining through the darkness of the year's midnight; Easter greets the light of the new dawning and the healing wings; Pentecost, however, finds the year at midday with the sun, 'busy old fool', at its zenith in mid-career. It is now, at the height of our powers, in the full maturity of our days, that we most need the clear light of wisdom, love and power.

It is as if the Spirit summoned the Church to join in the elemental dance. There is no force as destructive or as necessary to life as water. For those Jews of the Diaspora it provided a clear way to respond; as for Naaman and John Baptist it symbolized in a deceptively simple action, the process of renewal – 'Go and get washed!' Baptism, with its demand to repent and be transformed by the renewing of our minds, has symbolized ever since God's New Deal for humankind, rehearsed and recalled as we wash and greet every morning as the first day of the rest of our life.

Like water, wind conveys the image of renewal and refreshment as well as judgment. It breaks down barriers and knows no frontiers, carrying all before it. It separates wheat from chaff; but it also sweeps across the Valley of Dry Bones, shaking the skeletons of dryasdust institutions and finding new purposes for creaking, antiquated machinery. Because it blows where it will it finds prophets in strange places – Olaf Palme and Fritz Schumacher, Brecht and Picasso, to set beside a Wesley or a Pope John whom we have canonised and made our own. Even Islam and the exotic cults of California and Katmandu are pointing prophetic fingers at the decadent, materialistic West. We hear the sound thereof but cannot always tell what it means or where it is sending us.

But fire is the element that dictates the Pentecostal dance and red is its dominant colour. Flames give light and warmth, but they burn and leave ineradicable scars.

The images Pentecost evokes are those of power: the elemental forces of water, wind and fire.

The dove descending breaks the air
With flame of incandescent terror
Of which the tongues declare
The one discharge from sin and error.
The only hope, or else despair
Lies in the choice of pyre or pyre –
To be redeemed from fire by fire.[15]

That uncomfortable word of Jesus, 'I am come to set fire to the earth and I would it were already kindled', is echoed by the apocryphal saying, 'He that is near me is near the fire.' We cannot forget that he who was 'Ultimate Fire' was executed on a rubbish-tip and drew attention to that other tip, Gehenna, with its smoking bonfires (Mark 9, 44). Indeed, we may recall that when the early Fathers tried to describe the union of humanity and divinity in Christ they used the image of fire infusing itself with iron.

What astonishes us in those first Apostles is their unquenchable courage – the 'fire in their bellies'; a small group, initially dismissed as cranks and eccentrics, dangerous heretics, defying the world. What won the hearts of onlookers and confounded their enemies was their warmth, the friendship and mutual support we find and admire in many charismatic groups and significant revivalist movements (like the Focolare Movement) of our day. The Pentecostal fire welded the cultural and linguistic divisions into one invincible movement; but they still had to learn the cost of that transition from the old 'peculiar people' to the new. If the Christ who breathed his Spirit on them first showed them his wounded hands and feet, they too would carry those scars, as he had warned them. If 'he that is near me is near the fire', then those who cannot stand its heat had best stay out of the kitchen!

So the warning and the invitation remain; like those lukewarm Laodiceans, 'neither cold nor hot', we are still invited to join in the elemental dance and the Pentecostal banquet: 'Look, I am standing at the door, knocking. If one of you hears me calling and opens the door, I will come in to share his meal, side by side with him.' Today, the old 'Whitsun Ale' Agape-feasts after the Eucharist have become more sober and respectable Parish Breakfasts. The Lord of Misrule, chosen to preside over 'the Church Ale', attended by Fool and Mace-Bearer, has been banished to the pub next door; the hobby-horses have been hijacked by the children; the Morris dancing has been gentrified and folksyfied and is now performed by specialised groups like the White Horse Morris Men or The Dorset Triumph Folk Dancers, cross-gartered in their immaculate whites, waving their hankies like African politicians.

One old custom characteristic of the season, however, thrives throughout the land: the Mystery or Miracle Plays, performed usually on drays in the open air, originally by the different guilds of craftsmen. Today, while the National Theatre Company surprised every critic with its powerful and imaginative production of the York Cycle of Mystery Plays, they are usually performed by local people, untrained amateurs, occasionally directed by professionals. What such an experience can mean – with that unique blend of timeless truth and earthy humour ('eternity in love with the productions of time') – has been dramatically conveyed by James Roose-Evans, who was asked one year to direct the Chester Mystery Plays.

'I designed,' he writes, 'a large circular stage from the centre of which rose a thirty-foot-high pine tree, its branches lopped off to short stumps, but leaving some greenery at the top. This was the Cosmic Tree, the axis between heaven and earth, down which Lucifer climbed at the start. Hung with baskets of apples it became the Tree of Knowledge of Good and Evil; it served as a mast for the Ark, and at the end of the first half, when Mary entered the Temple for Simeon to bless the Child, it was hung with evergreen wreaths and storm lanterns, becoming a giant Christmas Tree. In the second half it became the cross . . . '[16]

LIVING IN TRINITY

It is part of the genius of the Mystery Plays that they present, almost in the form of majestic cartoons, the whole cosmic drama of Creation, Redemption and Fulfilment or, as with the National Theatre production, Nativity, Passion and Doomsday: 'Ego sum alpha et omega . . . '

> I am gracious and great, God withouten beginning;
> I am maker unmade, all might is in me.
> I am life and way unto wealth winning;
> I am foremost and first; als I bid shall it be . . .

And at the end:

Now is fulfilled all my forethought
For ended is all earthly thing.
All worldly wights that I have wrought
After their deeds have their dwelling . . . [17]

Presenting them at or around Whitsun we find the world in the full flowering of early Summer. We can look out at that world through the great arch rising from its twin pillars of Christmas and Easter: the coping-stone that holds it all in place and frames Truth in trinitarian form follows hard on the heels of Whitsun. It is not clear quite why the English Church, certainly from the time of Becket (and possibly before him) and the Western Church a century later, came to honour the Blessed Trinity with its own special Festival. The Orthodox, since the time of Chrysostom and the Emperor Leo, have celebrated what we know as 'Trinity Sunday' as the Festival of all the Martyrs.

At the close of the complete cycle from Advent to Whitsun, Trinity Sunday brings us up with a full stop and a warning. At Ascensiontide we were caught up in God's glory as Jesus was wrapped in the 'shekinah'. Now we are reminded of the supreme mystery at the heart of things.

> I saw the Lord . . . high and lifted up and his train filled the Temple . . . (Isa. 6, 1)

> After this I looked and, behold, a door was opened in Heaven . . . (Rev. 4, 1)

It is the Festival of all true iconoclasts, warning us that 'behind God is God'; 'This is Thou – yet is not this Thou.' All the great truths that we proclaim in our Creeds are at best models of truth; maps to point us in the right direction, not the landscape itself. Images, words, pictures, stories, statements are all necessary, since it is better to say something than to say nothing. But if we forget their symbolic nature and function we are but fools rushing in where angels (and the Angelic Doctor) fear to tread.

A small child, taken to the London Zoo for the first time, is shown a rhinoceros. He looks at the absurd shape of its nose, its fantastic horn, its eyes in the wrong place, its skin hanging down in wrinkled baggy folds like a dosser with too many overcoats. He stands for a long time in silent wonder, then looks up at his mother and asks: 'Why?'[18] It is the deepest, wisest, most profound question he can ask; but it takes a child, who alone can ask why the Emperor has no clothes, to ask it. If we pursue the question far enough and are not distracted on the way by the 'What?' or the 'How?' question, we arrive at something like the Ontological Argument, which may or may not satisfy the intellect with its quest for meaning, a First Cause or a significant purpose. But to 'acknowledge the glory of the eternal Trinity and in the power of the divine majesty to worship the Unity' requires the single-mindedness of the mystic or the uninhibited persistence of the child; which may explain why the First Beatitude commends the pure in heart, and why Jesus in an ecstatic moment ('filled with joy by the Holy Spirit' – Luke 10, 21) thanked the Father 'for hiding these things from the learned and clever and revealing them to mere children.'

The sense of mystery and wonder innate in a child is a gift as easy to sentimentalise as it is criminal to destroy. That time, immortalised by Traherne, when 'all appeared New and Strange at first, inexpressibly rare and Delightful and Beautiful. I was a little Stranger, which at my Entrance into the World was Saluted and Surrounded with innumerable Joys. My Knowledge was Divine, I knew by Intuition those things which, since my Apostasie, I Collected again by the Highest Reason. My very Ignorance was advantageous. I seemed as one Brought into the Estate of Innocence. All Things were Spotless and Pure and Glorious: yea, and infinitely mine, and Joyfull and Precious . . . I was entertained like an Angel with the Works of God in their Splendour and Glory, I saw all in the Peace of Eden; Heaven and Earth did Sing my Creator's Praises, and could not make more Melody to Adam than to me. All Time was Eternity, and a Perpetual Sabbath. Is it not Strange, that an Infant should be Heir of the whole world, and see those mysteries which the Books of the Learned never unfold? The corn was Orient and Immortal Wheat, which never could be reaped, nor was ever sown . . . '[19]

The child learns, with maturity, the difference between mystery (truth waiting to be revealed) and magic (truth extorted to manipulate, distorted to deceive people). And much of the learning comes through the use of models. Truth, we say, is *like* that; it is analogical. We learn to look at the supreme model, in the person of Christ, and affirm that the Way, Truth and Life are *like* that. It is like, in Dante's incomparable vision of the paradiso, 'the Love that moves the sun and the other stars.'

Many of the great Christian mystics and thinkers, like Augustine, have pointed to the Trinitarian model as we perceive it in human experience. To look at another is to engage in a Trinitarian exercise; the one who looks requires an object to be looked at and the sight which relates subject to object. The lover cannot be that without the beloved object and the love itself which binds them together. The building requires foundations to stand on, walls to contain space and a roof to complete it and define the area. Dorothy Sayers, in her 'Mind of the Maker' made great play of the Divine Architect model and described the aesthetic experience as a Trinitarian exercise.

In fact, all our prayers, however fumbling and perfunctory, are essentially Trinitarian: to the Father, through the Son (having the mind of Christ, using his prayer), in the Holy Spirit who leads us step by faltering step into all Truth, if we have the simplicity and openness to allow ourselves to be carried. The models, including the model prayer, may help and even illuminate; if they do not make sense we have to find others to which we can more readily respond. One man's rationality will be another man's rhinoceros. And it may or may not be encouraging to recall that the most rational of philosophers, Thomas Aquinas, refused to finish his 'Summa Theologica' at the end of his life; after a vision he had while celebrating Mass he is reputed to have said: 'Everything I have written seems worthless by the side of what I have seen.'

FIRE & WATER

As with the Feast of Trinity, there is a clear theological rationale behind the placing of the Festival of John the Baptist at the heart of the year. Of course, if John was six months older than Jesus, there was reason enough for placing his birthday on June 24th. But Augustine is probably nearer the truth when he points to the words, 'He must increase, but I must decrease.' 'John was born today,' he says, 'and from today the days decrease; Christ was born on the eighth of the kalends of January, and from that day the days increase.'

It is no accident to find the Baptist associated with the summer solstice; and no mere reactionary tactic, as if the Church wished to douse the bonfires with the waters of baptism. Midsummer finds the year in its full maturity, with the sun at full strength. So John must have seen in his cousin the coming of age of Messiah; it was the mark of his own maturity that he could direct attention away from himself and the old dispensation to the arrival of the new. Certainly, he was recognised as a true prophet in the great succession, Elijah redivivus; one who had the courage to swim against the stream, 'constantly to speak the truth, boldly rebuke vice and patiently suffer for the truth's sake.'

A measure of his stature is to be found, not simply in Jesus' own tribute to him ('a prophet and more than a prophet'), but in the survival of his movement well into the apostolic age. Paul and his fellow-missionaries would find pockets of his followers who 'knew only the baptism of John'. But his true stature and the mark of his supreme maturity is to be found in a blend of strong conviction and altruistic humility, a combination rare in prophets and leaders of popular movements. Like Elijah passing on his mantle to Elisha, he could generously acknowledge his own demise and welcome gladly the dawn of a new era, another 'sun'.

Around the festivities of Midsummer Day there is a tinge of sadness, a touch of magic and of menace, as the sun in mid-career begins its slow descent. The crowds who flocked to Shakespeare's plays knew that this was a time for dreams and enchantment, when Oberon and Titania would play havoc with the wills and affections of mere mortals. Similarly, the campers at Stonehenge in our day are aware of participating in a rite twice as old as Christianity, addressed to their deepest hopes and fears. If this is the longest day, from now on the shadows will begin to lengthen and Autumn must be kept at bay. Our ancestors pushed it back with their bonfires and fireworks, lightening the darkness of their forebodings; just as, at the winter solstice, the candles of Lucy's Day banished the darkness of long December nights and brought the hope of new light and longer days.

The Church sought to counteract the universal attraction of midsummer fires with its own celebration of water and water-baptism. It could draw on all the natural associations of sun, water and fire with fertility; as before in ancient Babylon, the image of Tammuz, 'the true son of the deep water', was bathed in water at the summer solstice, so the revellers who had lit their bonfires on Midsummer Eve would bathe themselves in the dew at sunrise and could now baptise Midsummer Day with the Festival of the baptiser himself. John Donne's prayer that 'thy Son may shine/As he shines now and heretofore' echoes an earlier play on the theme of Sun/Son:

> Lo, the Day-Spring   brightest angel
> sent to men   over this middle-earth,
> soothfast beam   of the very Sun,
> more bright than stars – Thou Thyself
> givest light forever   to time going by.
> As Thou, God,   begotten of God,
> true Son of the Father,   in sky's glory
> without beginning   forever wert,
> now in its need   Thine own handiwork
> begs Thee boldly   that Thou bring upon us
> that bright sun,   and come Thyself
> to enlighten swiftly   those who long since,
> wrapped in mist   and in murk darkness,
> sat through a long night,   sin-enfolded.[20]

A glimpse of the shining of that sun, the radiance of his glory, would be given on the Mount of Transfiguration.

NOTES

2. The metaphor of the 'loss of the stable state' was used by the American business psychologist, Donald Schon, in his Reith Lectures of 1970. It was taken up by J.A.T. Robinson in the opening chapter of 'The Difference in Being a Christian Today' (Fontana, 1972); he was, however, sceptical about any simple application to persons and institutions of processes in the world of inorganic matter, 'if only because while we are being changed we can reflect on the change as it were from outside it' (p. 13).
2. H.A. Williams, 'True Resurrection', Mitchell Beazley, 1972, pp. 11–12.

From 'New Fire', Vol. VIII, No. 58, Spring 1984, p. 24.

Sermon on his wife's death, 1752, from 'Selections from Samuel Johnson', ed. R.W. Chapman, World's Classics, OUP, 1962, p. 149. He goes on to add, 'But so much is our condition improved by the gospel, so much is the sting of death rebated, that we may now be invited to the contemplation of our mortality, as to a pleasing employment of the mind, to an exercise delightful and recreative, not only when calamity and persecution drive us out from the assemblies of men, and sorrow and woe represent the grave as a refuge and an asylum, but even in the hours of the highest earthly prosperity, when our cup is full, and when we have laid up stores for ourselves.'

Jacques Pohier, 'God in Fragments', SCM 1985, pp. 111–12.

Her comments were made in a Foreword to Raymond Moody's 'Life After Life', Bantam, USA, 1975. Thus Virgil is Dante's guru and guide in the Divine Comedy and George Macdonald is the 'significant religious figure' who acts as guide in C.S. Lewis' witty and profound novel about Purgatory, 'The Great Divorce'.

H.A. Williams, 'True Resurrection', p. 180–1.

James Roose-Evans, 'Inner Journey, Outer Journey', Hutchinson, 1987, p. 160.

I owe this reference and much besides to Pamela Tudor-Craig and her illuminating study of Uccello's 'St George and the Dragon' in 'The Secret Life of Paintings', Boydell Press 1986, pp. 25–39.

L. Whistler, 'The English Festivals', Heinemann, 1947, p. 152.

This Rogation Collect first appeared in Cosin's Devotions, 1626.

See particularly his Sermon 272 for his characteristic theme: 'Simus quod accipimus'. 'If you are the Body of Christ and his members, it is the sacrament of yourselves (mysterium vestrum) that is set upon the Lord's Table, the sacrament of ourselves that you receive. Be what you receive, and receive what you are.'

On the danger of 'systems that become ends in themselves', see John Bowker, 'Licensed Insanities', DLT 1987, Appendix on 'Religions as Systems', where he warns us against 'institutional imperialism': 'The systematic nature of systems is undoubtedly open to abuse and exploitation. All too easily the system becomes the end in itself. The responsibility of all Christians, in any generation, is to transform – or to allow God to transform through them – the dry bones of the system into a living presence which in turn touches, heals, restores, sustains many lives far beyond its own . . . ' (p. 142).

Kenneth Leech, 'True God', Sheldon SPCK, 1985, p. 383.

The 'cloud' that 'hid him from their sight' is most probably Luke's way of saying that Jesus entered the 'shekinah' (cloud) of the presence of God. In Rabbinic thought, the term 'shekinah', like the term 'glory', was used as a circumlocution for God himself, 'a reverent equivalent for God' (viz. art. on 'Presence', Theological Word Book of the Bible, ed. Alan Richardson, SCM, 1957, p. 176).

The 'shekinah' was the source of God's glory, as it was glimpsed on the Mount of Transfiguration (Viz, 2 Pet. 1, 17–8). Sayings like 'when two sit together and are occupied with the words of the Law, the shekinah is with them': 'the man is not without the woman nor the woman without the man, nor both of them without the Shekinah' would now have concrete reference to the personal presence of Christ. (Matt. 18, 20; 1 Cor. 11, 11)

15. T.S. Eliot, Little Gidding IV, from the 'Four Quartets'.
16. Roose-Evans, op. cit. p. 62. He applies to the life of the Church some words for Peter Brook: 'The search today is for a necessary theatre, one which is an urgent presence in our lives, speaking to its audience at a depth of feeling that precedes the dissection of man into social and psychological categories, *speaking to a man in* his wholeness' (his itals) (p. 67).
17. Taken from the opening and closing speeches of 'The Mysteries', adapted by Tony Harrison, Faber, 1985.
18. I am unable to trace the source of this anecdote. Philip Toynbee called formal creeds and dogmas 'a sort of metaphysical stutter'.
19. Thomas Traherne, 'Felicities', ed. Quiller-Couch, Dobell 1934, p. 11.
20. Cynewulf, a Northumbrian poet of the 8th Century.

5

Harvest Home

The leaves are falling, falling as from far,
as though above were withering farthest gardens;
they fall with a denying attitude.

And night by night, down into solitude,
the heavy earth falls far from every star.

We are all falling. This hand's falling too –
all have this falling-sickness none withstands.

And yet there's One whose gently-holding hands
this universal falling can't fall through.

(Rainer Maria Rilke)

Whatever else we worship from time to time, most of us in our semi-pagan hearts secretly worship the sun. Not that we actually think of a sun-god, like our Greek and Roman ancestors; or necessarily prostrate ourselves in naked adoration like the Scandinavians on the Costa Brava. To be secret sun-worshippers means that the sun makes everything seem worth while; it adds worth-ship to the world, brings colour and magic where before was monochrome monotony. It is no surprise that one of the largest British travel companies is called 'Intasun' which, with its fine fleet of Boeings, markets sea, sun and sand as skilfully as some sell second-hand cars.

It is very hard to be utterly gloomy or defeatist when the sun sheds a shaft of hope and warmth, putting despondency to flight. Partly because the body and the spirit are so firmly bound up together that the warmth outside kindles a kind of interior warmth; and not to respond seems ungrateful and insensitive. So I confess to being in some measure a fairweather believer. True, I may not work so well in summer, but I pray a good deal more fervently: I feel more at one with the world and myself. 'The world is charged with the grandeur of God,' says Hopkins, 'It will flame out like shining from shook foil . . . ' But this flaming is a fleeting, precarious thing – summer's lease hath all too short a date. The leaves start browning almost before the fruit ripens. And this elation, ecstasy, sense of wonder and the glory of it all has all too short a date as well. Happiness is a knife-edge thing: no sooner caught than on the wing again. So we store up the good moments with our Instamatics – click, click – like so many squirrels storing up nuts to last through the coming cold of winter.

Of all the seasons of the human spirit, high summer brings the sharpest note of warning. This sun I am basking in has not been earned, manufactured; it is a grace, something given:

> No price is set on the lavish summer,
> June may be had by the poorest comer.

The sun shines on the just and on the unjust. So I need not preen myself too proudly in my borrowed plumes.

It also brings its own lethargy, a dip in the energy supply, when the tensions of spring and autumn are relaxed and there is no sense of urgency. It is a season of middle-age, thickening round the gut. The Psalmist speaks of 'the sickness that destroyeth in the noon-day', the lethargy (what the mediaeval writes called 'accidie') that overtakes us in the middle years. The danger comes not so much from 'the peril by night, the pestilence that walketh in darkness': those fears may serve to keep us alert and vigilant. The danger comes when we are feeling relaxed, sleeping in the sun, in a false sense of security. Or when, as in that state of accidie, nothing seems to matter very much, and even our successes (such as they are) turn to dust and ashes in the mouth. And this sense of insouciance, the worldly-wisdom of middle-age, the listlessness that saps energy and drains all causes of their enthusiasm and youthful commitment, may be a trap preventing me from caring enough to take effective action. Or it may be pointing me on to the next stage, the fulfilment that comes with autumn and maturity. 'Teach us to care and not to care': above all, teach us to care for the things that really matter.

It is the precariousness of summer, the shook-foil flash and glimpse of glory, that give the Feast of Transfiguration its particular poignancy. The three friends, Peter, James and John, that inner core of intimates who seem to have shared a knowledge of the mind of Christ, would later share his troubled mind in Gethsemane. Now they are invited to glimpse, if only for a moment, his true nature and destiny. Within the limitations of Incarnation that glory is for the most part hidden, as it is for the believer under the mundane forms of bread and wine.

As with all the great disclosure-events in the Gospels, the context is highly significant. The Synoptic writers (John, of course, does not record the Transfiguration) place it six days (Matthew and Mark) or 'about eight days' (Luke) after Jesus' solemn prediction: 'There are some standing here who will not taste death before they see the kingdom of God come with power.' In its turn, that prediction had followed Peter's confession at Caesarea Philippi and the first prophecy of the Passion. The truth is revealed – and apprehended – in successive layers of reality: who he is; what will happen to him; what his ultimate meaning and destiny may one day be perceived to be. And because he is New Adam and New Creation it is our meaning and destiny also. What had been a 'foretaste of the Kingdom' at the Transfiguration would become a fact for us his followers:

> What we are to be in the future has not yet been revealed,
> all we know is, that when it is revealed
> we shall be like him
> because we shall see him as he really is. (1 John, 3, 2)

But there is a further – and deeper – context. Truth is not revealed in a vacuum: it requires the most careful preparation if it is to be properly apprehended and not distorted: the research thorough, the ground uncluttered, the chalice open and the hands extended. The presence of Moses and Elijah, representing the Law and the Prophets, marks their contribution to the preparation-process. Moses had himself glimpsed God's glory and reflected it to his people; he had (as in the 'dream' of Martin Luther King) climbed the Mountain, looked over at the Promised Land but never entered it. Elijah also, that troubler of Israel and lonely champion of God's truth and justice, had heard the still small voice after the whirlwind and the thunder. And now the voice, the 'Bath Qol', marks out the Christ as the one to whom both Law and Prophets were pointing: 'Listen to him!'

Only Luke (9, 13) tells us anything of their discourse: 'they were speaking of his passing (exodus) which he was to accomplish in Jerusalem.' The first Exodus had liberated a people; the second would liberate the world. Sinai and Horeb meet on Mount Hermon. At such a moment of intersection, the meeting-place of history with historical fulfilment, it is no wonder the spectators were non-plussed. It seems that the moment of vision came in the course of a night spent in prayer and vigil; as later they were in a state between sleep and waking, totally unprepared for the mystical experience that the Petrine writer was later to describe as 'seeing his majesty for ourselves (2 Peter, 1, 16).'

For orthodox Jews the sign of God's presence in the 'shekinah' would naturally suggest the 'tent of meeting' in the wilderness (Exodus 33, 7–11). Peter's offer to build 'tabernacles' was not a random response ('he knew not what to say'), as Mark comments, but his way of handling a mystery totally beyond his experience; a means of protection, also, from the blinding light. Everyone knew that the Presence could be dangerous; like an electric charge it had been known to kill the hapless Uzziah who had only tried to steady the Ark on its bullock-cart (2 Samuel 6, 7)! Perhaps it was as much his way of taming, domesticating the Spirit by institutionalising it as it was a means of prolonging the ecstatic moment.

'Our life speaks true both of God and man,' writes John Robinson. 'For here he is reflected, defined and focused "as in a son". The partition between the servants' quarters and the master's part of the house is down. The veil is removed, the heavens opened, there is a point of transfiguration, a dwelling of the Shekinah among men, angels ascending and descending upon the Son of Man. In all these picturesque ways the New Testament writers seek to communicate the fact that in Jesus the transcendent has been for them uniquely visible "from below"; the meaning of the process has become translucent, luminous as sacrificial love. Here they have seen a window into God – at first hand: not just the love of human response but God coming through, not homoioagape, but homoagape.'[1]

In that ecstatic moment those friends of Jesus are privileged not only to glimpse his glory, but also, by virtue of his complete humanity, to share some perception of our own human destiny, 'the hope of glory'. In the words of Irenaeus, 'the glory of God is a living man; and the life of man is the vision of God.' It was a disclosure, a moment of truth that would be obscured and distorted by subsequent events, but not forgotten. Similarly with our own lesser 'illuminations', when it becomes momentarily clear 'what it's all about' – they fade, and we have constantly to be recalled and have our original vision renewed:

> I saw a door open in heaven and heard the same voice speaking to me, the voice like a trumpet saying 'Come up here: I will show you what is to come in the future.' (Revelation, 4, 1)

THE HUMAN PARADOX

The vision fades, and the friends are left alone with Jesus. They cannot stay, for another vision awaits them at the foot of the mountain, the writhing, hideous spectacle of the epileptic boy. From the vision of what human nature can become, of a world wrapped in the uncreated light, they now see in the harsh light of reality what human nature is actually like and what it has to endure. For us the contrast is presented by the light 'brighter than a thousand suns' that irradiated Hiroshima in 1945 on the very day, August 6, when the Church keeps Transfiguration. The paradox of 'l'homme, la gloire et le rébut de l'univers', this ambiguous earth, was tragically set forth on that momentous day when light shone and the darkness encompassed it. The figures of those three awestruck witnesses, depicted in Orthodox iconography tumbling down the hill of Hermon in confusion, shielding their eyes from the uncreated light, are inextricably linked in our minds with the victims of Hiroshima and Nagasaki, blinded by the monstrously created light of nuclear radiation. Since 1945, we cannot totally dissociate Transfiguration from the passage in the Bhagavad Gita which came into the mind of Robert Oppenheimer, Director of the Manhattan Project, at the first fateful flash of the atomic bomb in

Almagordo, New Mexico:

> If the radiance of a thousand suns
> were to burst into the sky,
> that would be like
> the splendour of the Mighty One.

And then, as the sinister mushroom cloud rose over Point Zero, he recalled another line from the same source. Krishna, the Exalted One, says:

> I am become Death, the shatterer of worlds.

That moment when the nuclear age was born was not merely burnt into the memories and consciousness of the scientists who were its midwives; it has cast a shadow over every human life and all living species, while opening up unimaginable opportunities for a creative future. 'It has not yet been revealed what we can become' – for good or ill.

But the horror of Hiroshima and that date, August 6, 1945, can never obscure the glory of a vision once perceived; indeed, that vision of Christ the Light of the World was itself part of the preparation for what was to follow. The inner circle was being warned of the approaching 'Exodus', and they were required to see Mount Hermon as pointing not back to Mount Sinai but forward to Mount Calvary. Transfiguration was both a 'Retreat', a moment out of time, a holiday enabling them to 'vacare Deo', give open space to God; it was also a teaching-opportunity, marking a new direction which would take Jesus from glory and illumination to darkness and an inglorious death.

> Now as the time drew near for him to be taken up to heaven, he resolutely took the road for Jerusalem and sent messengers before him. (Luke 9, 51)

When we use summer and take holidays in the company of close family and friends, we find the walls of habit and routine, our natural framework and reference-points, removed. We are presented with fresh opportunities for growth, deepened awareness and even illumination. New horizons restore our vision and give another direction, a better perspective for the next stage of the journey. Because we have been removed from the familiar landscape with those mundane supports and sign-posts we take largely for granted, we can be gently prepared for the possibly painful and stretching development that is being demanded of us, as it was of those companions of Christ as they descended from the mountain and set out together on the road to Jerusalem and the Passion.

Late summer, with its tang of mist and smell of burning stubble, brings both a sense of fulfilment, the harvested hopes, and also a touch of sadness. The earth is beginning to die back into itself, taking back some of the life it gave to crops and trees.

> Not for ever by green pastures do we ask our way to be,
> But the steep and ragged pathway may we tread rejoicingly.
>
> Not for ever by still waters would we idly rest and stay,
> But would smite the living fountains from the rocks along our way . . .

Life 'on the plain', returning to the familiar landmarks, both boring and reassuring, will never be the same. But it can now be lived, as faith has been described, 'on the evidence of its highest moments'. The light that shone on Moses' face, as he descended from Mount Sinai and his own highest moment of ecstatic communion with his God, would not remain; but it made it possible for him and his people to press on with their journey through the desert. The glimpse of glory, hints of the transcendent, which we occasionally perceive along the way, provide sufficient encouragement to continue our personal journey. Dominus Illuminatio Mea . . .

> The Lord is my light and my salvation,
> whom then shall I fear?
> The Lord is the stronghold of my life,
> of whom shall I be afraid?

(Psalm 27)

The approach of autumn turns our minds to Harvest Thanksgiving, the crown of all those other festivals which speak of earth and our responsibility towards it – Plough Sunday, Rogationtide, Lammas. The crowds who give vent to 'We plough the fields and scatter . . . ', the children who bring a tin of baked beans or a handful of Michaelmas daisies owe much to Parson Hawker, the Cornish vicar of Morwenstow, who revived ancient customs and dressed them, as Eric Milner-White did with his Festival of Nine Lessons and Carols, in new clothes. Many of these customs had been secular; a way of celebrating weeks of hard work in the fields and (in the days before silos and insurance) victory over the climatic hazards of an English August/September.

> We have ploughed, we have sowed,
> We have reaped, we have mowed,
> We have brought home every load,
> Hip, hip, hip, Harvest Home!

These, in their turn, are indebted to the Jewish feast of Succah or Tabernacles (Deuteronomy 16). Israel is being asked to remember the two basic scriptural truths of Dependence and Dominion: our dependence on God and interdependence with each other, on the one hand; his entrusting to us of dominion over and stewardship for all creation on the other.

The first truth is easier to forget in an urban than in a rural environment. When milk comes from bottles and water from taps it is easy to imagine, in the event of shortage, that we only have to order more or turn on harder. The offertory prayer at the heart of the Orthodox Liturgy expresses it in words that stem from Solomon's prayer: 'Ta sa ek ton son soi prospheromen' (Thine own of Thine own we bring to Thee) and are reflected in our own Liturgy: 'All things come from you, and of your own do we give you.' A proper sense of dependence protects us from the arrogance of supposing that technology by itself – or economic planning by itself – will solve the central problem of our day, the just distribution of the world's resources. The shelves of Africa Hall, in Addis Ababa, the centre for the UN Economic Commission for Africa, are stacked with Five Year, Ten Year Plans for agricultural and industrial development which have done little over the years to halt the seemingly inexorable advance of deserts and dust-bowls across the Continent.

It is said that at the outbreak of a terrible plague in Constantinople the Patriarch announced that this was a judgment on the wickedness of their people and called on them to make a special act of penitence. Not unreasonably so, in the face of the gross inefficiency and complacency that marked Byzantine bureaucracy. However, one of the city's doctors pointed to a particular piece of wickedness: they had not looked after the drains. It would not help, he said, if they simply fell on their knees and failed to unblock the drains and improve the system of sanitation. What appears to us as commonsense was too secular a solution for the Byzantines: the doctor was imprisoned for impiety. But he was, in fact, giving expression to the second great truth that God has given us Dominion. As Marx would say, it is not enough to understand the world (or wring our hands over its injustices) – our responsibility is to change it. Without an active, dynamic acknowledgment of the summons to exercise dominion ('Subdue the earth . . . ') dependence can decline into fatalism.

It may have been Marx's Jewish background which lent weight to his celebrated critique of religion as a drug. For centuries the Jewish people had never been in control of their destiny; they had been at the mercy of pogroms, expulsions, persecution at the hands of the Gentile world. One rabbi lamented that 'Gentile kings are like the weather – you just have to put up with them.' A fatalism induced by centuries of persecution made it easier for the Nazis to herd them into cattle-trucks and despatch them in their millions. 'Heaven is for birds and Christians,' said Hitler, 'the earth is for us.' This is, of course, to ignore the prophetic witness within Judaism which found in religion not a drug to ease the pain and make suffering tolerable, but a dynamic incitement to remove the causes of that suffering. It was the God of Justice who told Elijah, 'the troubler of Israel', to confront King Ahab in Naboth's vineyard and purge the land of Jezebel and all her works. The mantle of Elijah has fallen on all those, from John the Baptist to Romero, Tuto and the Liberation Theologians of our day who would willingly accept Marx's critique of *bad* religion but reject his interpretation of *all* religion. To hold together the two truths of Dependence and Dominion should protect us from falling victims of arrogance or despair. The presence within society of centres of resistance resolved to 'obey God rather than men' should not merely comfort the oppressed but acutely discomfort the oppressor. Niebuhr's great prayer holds both together: for the patience to accept the things that cannot be changed (dependence), but also the power to change the things that can (dominion) – 'and the wisdom to know the difference'.

CARE OF CREATURES

That dominion is given to be exercised not only over the earth and its products but over all creatures (Genesis 1, 26). It is not enough to hold a balanced theological/ecological view of the world if this is at the expense of all the creatures entrusted to Adam to name, identify and nurture. The biblical picture of Adam the Gardener, Man/Woman in harmony with each other and with all creation, has never been surpassed. In Keith Ward's paraphrase:

> So the first man and the first woman lived together and cared for the garden of bliss and all the animals in the garden, and found their delight in one another without shame or fear. In the time of innocence they walked with God in the garden, and all things gave praise to their creator.[3]

Scripture gives us a similar picture of the Hebrew 'shalom' with the establishment of peace and justice when the lion lies down with the lamb and all flesh shall see God's glory. This is the Kingdom in all its fullness which Christ, the Second Adam, came to proclaim with its new beginning, the year of Jubilee (Luke 4, 18–19), quoting Isaiah 61, 2, the proclamation of a 'year of favour').

Unhappily, what was intended to be united humans have separated: Christian spirituality has connived at an artificial separation of the natural and the 'supernatural'. The natural, material world has been seen not as a bridge carrying us over to the world of the Spirit, incarnating grace and reflecting the glory and grandeur of God; but rather as a barrier, blocking our view, an obstacle to be overcome or circumvented and a distraction from the things of the Spirit. Kenneth Leech remarks of Thomas à Kempis' 'Imitation of Christ', which generations of Christians have taken as their spiritual guide, that it has been influential in teaching that 'in order to come close to God, one must withdraw more and more from creatures . . . The notion that creatures and material things are a block and a barrier to experience of God remains widespread in Christian circles, and it is difficult to see the influence of à Kempis' book as other than damaging in this regard.'[4]

Such a negative, world-denying attitude contrasts sharply with the universalist spirit of St Francis and his Canticle of the Sun:

> Be thou praised, my Lord, with all thy creatures . . . for our sister, Mother Earth, who sustains us and holds us to her breast, and produces abundant fruits, flowers and trees . . .

Because it was combined with an intense personal asceticism and austerity his universalism was prevented from becoming sentimental or romantic. Francis was expressing a sublime unity with all creatures not in spite of but because of his unity and constant communion with God. Aquinas gave this philosophical expression when he taught that God creates myriads of other beings to reflect the mystery of his own Being; thus, the whole universe reflects his goodness more perfectly than any particular thing and all species are necessary for his perfection.[5]

Separation from the world and dissociation from creatures give carte blanche to those intent on making vast tracts of the world totally uninhabitable; who would pour acid rain over Europe and Scandinavia; decimate and raze to the ground the vast rain-forests of S. America and make lakes and oceans radio-active, contaminated, dead. By making humanity the centre we have connived at the plundering and pillaging of Planet Earth and the disappearance, perhaps for all time, of its many-splendoured species. Not because we are particularly or spectacularly wicked: the problems are caused not simply by greedy capitalists, pirates intent on quick profits and easy pickings, but by good people who promise a wonder-world through the benefits of industry, nuclear power, mass-production and undreamed of sources of energy. What they deliver are simply the dreams, the beautiful brochures of the world of advertising, together with a decaying infra-structure of motorways, drains, tower-blocks, hospitals and municipal palaces of variety that can only be maintained at immense cost.

The task for our generation is to replace the homocentric with the geocentric view. We have shown ourselves to be sensitive to the needs of the poor (however inadequately we address those needs); we must show ourselves equally sensitive to the needs of earth and its species. We are clear about the evils of homicide and suicide: we must be equally clear about geocide and biocide.[6] It would be tragic indeed if our obsession with economic solutions distracted us from the underlying ecological crisis which must be resolved if any economy in North or South is to survive. It would be equally tragic and ultimately futile if we at last resolved our Cold War conflicts, dismantled our stock-piles and found that we had bequeathed to our grandchildren merely the peace and emptiness of a vast desert. In the words of the Roman historian, Tacitus: 'Desertam faciunt, pacem appellant – they make a desert and call it peace!' We in the Judaeo–Christian tradition who work and pray for shalom, peace on earth, must equally work and pray for peace *with* earth and all its creatures. To this end we must re-tell the story of Adam the Gardener, Dominion and Stewardship. Only by rediscovering the insights of Genesis shall we effect the Exodus, the true liberation of the hungry and oppressed, the wretched of the earth.

Paradoxically, it may well be that in this task Darwin, who is always considered the great debunker of the Genesis story, might be enlisted as a valuable ally. For it is Darwin's emphasis on the close links between humans and the animal kingdom and the attention he and other naturalists draw to the uniqueness of every (and not merely the human) species that may rescue them from their threatened extinction. Nearly twenty years ago, Max Nicholson, the conservationist, accused Christians of 'obstructing the way to harmony between man and nature':

> Deriving its earliest inspiration from the wilderness, Christianity has signally failed to bear witness to its indebtedness and to teach the need for respect towards what it professes to regard as the works of its Creator. Only during the past few years, under pressure from outside, have there been any signs within the churches of interest in evaluating and reviving vital elements of Christian tradition which have been increasingly neglected since

> the days of St Francis of Assisi. To develop a debate within the churches on the theological contribution to the problem of man's place in nature, and on the churches' obligation to speak up against the violations of man's responsibilities in this field, must be listed high among the background requirements which are overdue to be met.[7]

Since then, the churches have begun to respond, however inadequately, to the challenge of the Green Revolution. It is, however, no more than a first step to understand and theologise about the threat to our eco-system. If we are to ensure a just, peaceful and sustainable way of life (for ourselves, no less than for the impoverished two-thirds of the world's population) will demand a fundamental change in the values, lifestyles and institutions of the richer nations. 'Think globally, act locally', 'Live simply that others may simply live' must be the dominant slogans not just of pressure-groups and the Ecology Party, but of all Parties.

What is unforgivable and self-defeating is for the prophets of doom to place a load of unrelieved guilt on the shoulders of people who feel totally impotent to change the system. It is certainly incumbent on all of us to know the facts, stark and inescapable, and the options before us; it has been too easily assumed that some magical solution – Social Credit, the I.M.F., World Government or World Anything – will resolve the deepening crisis and rescue Third World populations from the poverty trap. All the Aid agencies are aware that emergency measures, even concentration on long-term development, are merely palliatives. Indeed, there is good evidence that much of our bilateral 'aid' has done actual harm in burdening developing countries with debts they can never repay.

'We are seeing, through the payment of debt interest', said John Hatch in 1984, 'greater sums being paid from Third World countries to Europe than the total of overseas aid and investment going from Europe to these countries . . . In 1983 the net loss of Third World countries vis-a-vis the EEC countries was in the region of 21 billion dollars. I repeat that was the net loss.'[8] Cynics could say that this might bear out Jesus' observation (it could hardly be a prescription!) that 'to him that hath shall be given and from him that hath not shall be taken away even that which he hath.'

The task is essentially one for governments, international agencies, multi-national corporations and the banking system to undertake. But churches and the non-governmental aid agencies have an important, if subsidiary role in undertaking public education, puncturing complacency, making the true facts known and providing opportunities for individuals to make their own contribution; however small, to the alleviation of suffering and the establishment of a more just economic order. Without that safety-valve, we are plunged into a deepening despair and an overwhelming sense that we are not part of the solution but part of the problem.

GROWING GOLD

The approach of Autumn is marked by the musky tang of bonfires clearing away the last vestiges of Summer. The sheer beauty of its browns and golds is tempered by the first nip in the evening air: the feet going swish, swish through the fallen leaves. Doors and windows begin to close and we prepare our first line of defence against the invading draughts of Winter. No one can think of Autumn without Keats' 'Season of mists and mellow fruitfulness, Close bosom-friend of the maturing sun.' Maturity, ripeness is all. When Autumn comes we expect it to bring wisdom and to put everything into perspective. We may forgo the ecstasies of Spring; but at least we are no longer dancing up and down on a Yo-Yo between exhilaration and despair.

Maturity may degenerate into smugness and contentment into complacency. But it should bring a measure of self-knowledge: I know that I do not know and, above all, I know *what* I need not know. I do not have to keep up those elaborate pretence-mechanisms. Maturity strips off the masks and leaves me vulnerable, exposed, but more secure in my real values. In some measure I have sorted out my priorities. It is the season of 'the fallen leaf, but it is also a wider horizon more clearly seen. It is the distant hills once more in sight, and the enduring constellations above them once again.' The vistas which Summer and its engrossing activity had blocked are now open: I can see life steadily and see it whole.

Keats wrote his celebrated 'Ode to Autumn' ten days before Michaelmas, imagining himself seated 'by a cider-press, with patient look, watching the last oozings hours by hours.' He tells his friend, Reynolds, how he came to write it:

'How beautiful the season is now – how fine the air. A temperate sharpness about it. Really, without joking, chaste weather – Dian skies – I never liked stubble-fields so much as now – Aye better than the chilly green of the Spring. Somehow a stubble-plain looks warm – in the same way that some pictures look warm. This struck me so much in my Sunday's walk that I composed upon it.'[9]

GETTING THE MESSAGE

The festival of Michaelmas itself, at least as old as the Fourth Century, has been overshadowed by the popularity of Harvest Thanksgivings. We no longer eat goose on the day (or give up a goose with the quarterly rent, as our mediaeval ancestors did) and its name largely survives to mark an academic Term or linked with the universal, innocuous daisy. But it also serves to remind us of other dimensions of existence, 'the innumerable company of angels' (Hebrews 12, 22), 'the ministering spirits, sent forth to minister for them who shall be heirs of salvation' (1, 14). While we close some windows we open others to the many-splendoured thing, the presence of the whole company of heaven round our eucharistic altars. Francis Thompson, for whom the angels kept their ancient places, saw 'the traffic of Jacob's ladder pitched betwixt Heaven and Charing Cross', as William Blake before him saw Parliament Hill Fields wrapt in a vision of angels.

The poets were drawing on the ancient Hebrew belief that there exists within or behind the natural, visible world an order of being which occasionally invades or impinges upon it. In the Old Testament there is no clear-cut distinction between natural and supernatural: theophany is not exactly an everyday event, but God is expected to make himself known, to visit his people and even (as in the apparition to Abraham at Mamre, celebrated by Rublev's greatest icon) eat with them. But their function, as the name angelos (messenger) implies, was to bring special communications and to provide particular protection. The theophany to Abraham (Genesis 18) or to Joshua (Josh. 5, 13) carries the authority of a divine mandate which cannot be denied or withstood.

Jesus seems to have accepted current Jewish belief in this 'other' order of being, just as he accepted – and exorcised – the presence of 'demons' and the invasion of the human and natural world by supernatural powers of evil. His comment, almost an aside, that children have their own guardian angels, protecting them in heaven

The messages are conveyed, the artistic or aesthetic inspiration is conferred, and we know the angels are still at work, tapping us on the shoulder and suggesting a new line of lateral thinking, a new hypothesis for investigation or research.

(Matt. 18, 10), serves to reinforce the unique value of even the weakest of creatures. Not surprisingly, children do not share our adult inhibitions over the presence of these intelligences. For them the Angel of Mons would be as conceivable an intervention as the angel with the drawn sword was to Joshua as he confronted Jericho. Their world is close to that of the novels of Charles Williams or C.S. Lewis where we are as likely to meet angels (or 'Eldrils') as we are to meet archetypal beasts or Platonic Forms. The everyday world of Kensington or Waterloo is invaded by the marvellous and our convenient frontiers between natural and supernatural are breached. Adults tend to leave angels to the poets and their

> Strong, still light upon the verge of Being,
> burning out into nocturnal space,
> while we spend ourselves in dimly-seeing
> hesitation round about your base.[10]

But all of us dream and experience in our dreams a similar 'invasion' where physical limitations are suspended. The living and the dead come together in the same world and neither space nor time can separate us from the overarching truth which we dare not face in our waking, fully conscious moments. Dreams perform for us the angelic function of communicating the wonderful or unpalatable truth, overlaid or suppressed by the censorious discipline of the conscious mind. The messages are conveyed, the artistic or aesthetic inspiration is conferred, and we know the angels are still at work, tapping us on the shoulder and suggesting a new line of lateral thinking, a new hypothesis for investigation or research.

> And something guiltily descried
> goes sometimes fluttering through their dream . . .
> until the waiting air engages
> their spread wings, when the wind they raise
> blows strong as though beyond the ages
> God's sculptor-fingers turned the pages
> in the dark book of first essays.[11]

As in the days of Abraham so today, the angels visit us not merely in ideas or inspiration but also in other people. 'Be not forgetful to entertain strangers,' warns the writer to the Hebrews, 'for thereby some have entertained angels unawares.' The neglected truth or other, suppressed half of the truth may be revealed in a dream or as a totally unlooked for imaginative leap, a special 'visitation'; but more probably through a chance meeting in a pub or a train. Whether 'surprised by joy' or finding the way unexpectedly blocked, like Balaam on his ass, we may later find that a maddening diversion has been unmasked as a providential dispensation.

'Scripture tells us,' writes B.F. Westcott, 'that messengers of God are about us on every side. The ministry of angels is the perfected type of our work. Are they messengers of God? So are we, charged to declare one to another the truth we know. Are they the sons of God? So are we, by the power which Christ has given us. Are they called the "watchers"? Such is the charge which the Lord has laid upon us . . .'[12]

THE GOOD COMPANIONS

Michaelmas past, the year is visibly ageing; it is, as some like to see the process, 'Growing Gold'. As dusk falls the mists and mellow fruitfulness dissolve into the wreathing smoke of bonfines consuming the last, damp, lingering leaves. The days close in and, with them, the memories. November could be a maudlin month, dedicated to St. Nostalgia, with All Saints, All Souls and Remembrance Day encouraging us to grieve over the snows – or the sunshine – of yesteryear. Où sont les neiges d'antan . . . ? It is the season in our own lifespan when the newly retired, or those preparing for retirement, are made to think of their mortality. They turn to researching into their genealogical roots and consult the records to construct a family tree. If retirement also involves moving home that makes the roots more, not less important; we need to know where we have come from, the old identity, before we can establish a new identity and plot the next stage of the journey.

But All Saints-tide need not encourage a mood of backward-looking nostalgia. We may be dogged by the ghosts of If-Only and What-Might-Have-Been which taunt us with delusory hopes, like the apple-bobbing games of Hallow-E'en. If we are subjected to the trials of 'Trick or Treat', when children place their victims in merciless 'Catch 22' dilemmas, we are reminded of those other tricks that Providence can play: 'the changes and chances of this mortal life', the roads not taken or which, when taken, turned out to be culs-de-sac.

When the Church decreed, as it did on November 1st, A.D. 608, that we should keep two days to remember 'the great multitude, which no man could number, of all nations and kindreds and people and tongues', it was recalling us to the slender line that divides the living and the dead, the orders of the natural and the supernatural. The echoes of the old pagan 'ghoulies and ghosties and things that go bump in the night' may linger on with many a sub-Christian stratum of popular superstition. Similarly, we may look back to the old heroes and the good companions, willing their return and wondering why they were snatched from us. Nostalgia can play its cruel 'if-only/what-if' games ad nauseam. 'If Only' Bonhoeffer or William Temple, Keats, Mozart, Edward Thomas or Wilfred Owen had been given another ten years! Is it simply 'those whom the gods love' who die young? Is it conceivable that we should think the same of St Joan or St Therese – let alone the young Carpenter of Nazareth – if their Spring and early Summer had been allowed to linger into Autumn? Snatched they may have been before due time; yet they are still with us and around us, the great cloud of witnesses, urging us on in the race for which we are entered, like the massed crowds of Wembley or Hampden Park. 'Knit together' with us, they are gathered up in the one Bread of Christ's mystical body.

Before thy throne we sinners meet
  As joint petitioners to thee;
In spirit we each other greet
  And shall again each other see.

So writes the Puritan, Richard Baxter, presenting us with a fine image of ships sailing over the horizon, lost to view, but waiting to greet us when we arrive ourselves in port:

As for my friends they are not lost,
  The several vessels of thy fleet;
Though parted now, by tempest tost,
  Shall safely in thy haven meet.

And so, to the angels and archangels of Michaelmas we must now add 'the whole company of heaven', those whom Charles Williams called the Companions of the Co-inherence, gathered round in the 'web of the glory'.

In other cultures, African, Indian and Chinese, this forms a natural, constant undercurrent to daily life. The ancestors are all around them, making the very earth holy with their presence. This makes even more intolerable the obscene scandal of enforced removal of whole communities under the Group Areas Act: the unforgivable rape of the Indian Territories by the pioneers and gold-prospectors of the Mid-West. The justly celebrated speech of the Dwamish Chief, Seattle, to Isaac Stevens, Governor of Washington Territory, in 1854, may convey the enormity of their loss:

> . . . To us the ashes of our ancestors are sacred and their resting-place is hallowed ground. You wander far from the graves of your ancestors and seemingly without regret . . . Our religion is the traditions of our ancestors – the dreams of our old men, given them in solemn hours of night by the Great Spirit . . . Your dead cease to love you and the land of their nativity as soon as they pass the portals of the tomb and wander way beyond the stars. They are soon forgotten and never return. Our dead never forget the beautiful world that gave them being . . . Every part of this soil is sacred in the estimation of my people. Every hillside, every valley, every plain and grove has been hallowed by some sad or happy event in days long vanished. The very dust upon which you now stand responds more lovingly to their footsteps than to yours, because it is rich with the blood of our ancestors and our bare feet are conscious of their sympathetic touch.

He warns the Governor that these invisible dead will remain 'still loving this beautiful land', so 'let him be just and deal kindly with my people, for the dead are not powerless. Dead, did I say? There is no death, only a change of worlds.' Half a century later, in 1909, at the Little Bighorn council grounds in Montana, the Crow Chief began his farewell address with a similar cry: 'The ground on which we stand is sacred ground. It is the dust and blood of our ancestors.'[13]

Indeed, the ancestors provide an important focus for traditional African religious and ritual and experience. The Dinka, says the anthropogist Lienhardt, offer them food and drink and imagine that these beings physically consume these offerings; they exercise a profound influence on the living, conferring wisdom, vitality, happiness and even status. Thus, when there is a dispute over a chieftaincy amongst the Ila people of Zambia, the candidate who can prove that he comes from a powerful ancestor has his case strengthened:

> My old friend Mungalo now sitting smoking a pipe with me, or sitting yonder under the eaves of his hut and carving a wooden spoon, is the Mungalo who lived here 100 years ago, and furthermore, Mungalo is his 'musedi', his guardian spirit, always accompanying him, guarding him, warning him of danger . . . [14]

The rites de passage, so carefully and thoughtfully conducted by Africans, contrast sharply with the clinical, perfunctory rites of our Western crematoria. Confined to a statutory twenty minutes, replete with canned music, buzzers, grinding machinery and verbal euphemisms (we must speak not of the dead but of the 'departed': not of death but of 'passing') – our 20th Century rituals provide little opportunity for the expression of natural grief, let alone the assurance of resurrection and continuing life. Children and grandchildren are often excluded, presumably on the grounds that we should not allow morbid thoughts to spoil the even tenor of their ways; even though children, above all, are notably realistic in their approach to death and can accept it more naturally and readily than adults. As we have already observed in relation to hospitals and hospices, our concern is to tidy the dead away, to separate the living from the dead in watertight compartments. So we refuse to recognise the powerful influence and continuing presence of 'the ancestors' over our lives. Perhaps there never was a time when we needed to think more deeply about the Communion of Saints and the Fellowship of All Souls.

HORIZONTAL & VERTICAL

All Saints-tide holds together two views of human life – the horizontal and the vertical which should never be separated:

One family we dwell in him,
  One church above, beneath;
Though now divided by the flood,
  The narrow stream of death.

The intersection of the horizontal and the vertical is found when we re-member the unity of the family of living and departed round the altar. Christ 'the firstborn of the dead' meets us, his new creation; we, by baptism, are alive in him and he in us. There is some affinity with the veneration of ancestors in other cultures, but an important difference: Easter and Resurrection. A friend recently returned from a visit to China, where he joined the crowds filing solemnly past the embalmed body of Chairman Mao, underlined the difference between the two traditions. 'The Chinese,' he said, 'worship the dead and the tomb is full; Christians worship the living and the tomb is empty.'

The reunion of friends with their living Lord is also, in the Communion of Saints, our reunion with friends who have gone gently into God's good night. The pain of loss and separation is still there, the aching void and vacuum of bereavement. It is not as if we were pretending they were here, summoned up like the dead Samuel by the witch of Endor, with us in the same room; rather that they are with us in the Father's house (John 14, 2), but in the next room. And 'Christ leads us through no darker rooms than he went through before.'

When W.R. Inge, 'the gloomy Dean' of St Paul's, wrote his book 'Personal Religion and the Life of Devotion', he had just lost his greatly loved nine year old daughter, Paula. He prefaced it with a poem: 'Weep not for her who has been snatched away; but learn to follow her.'

> Bereavement [he wrote] is the deepest initiation into the mysteries of human life – more searching and profound than even happy love. Love remembered and consecrated by grief belongs, more clearly than the happy intercourse of friends, to the eternal world: it has proved itself stronger than death. Bereavement is the sharpest challenge to our trust in God: if faith has overcome this, there is no mountain it cannot remove. And faith can overcome it.[15]

But All Saints-tide holds together not only two views of human life, but also two views of the Christian Church. The Catholic/Orthodox perspective is essentially hierarchical/vertical; authority devolves from above, and we the members are called out (as the word 'ecclesia' denotes) to bear witness to revealed truth. The Protestant perspective is essentially democratic/horizontal; authority is conferred by the community, the 'gemeinde' or company of the faithful, who find a common mind, elect their government and officers and commission their members to preach the Word and serve the world. Here the operative word is not so much 'ecclesia' but 'synagogue', the gathered community. It is a perspective which has been recovered by the 'Base Communities' among Latin American Catholics, with their 're-invention' of the Church.[16]

The two perspectives may be symbolised in architectural terms by the dome and the spire. The dome or sacred canopy represents truth overarching and enclosing our life in a sanctified space; the spire symbolises the human search for the transcendent, reaching out, striving higher and ever higher for fulfilment. They are not mutually exclusive, but mutually necessary to the whole view of authority which is never self-authenticating, wholly derived from below, but needs to be validated by that other source of truth which we call tradition. If we think that Vox Populi is always and inevitably Vox Dei we have only found for ourselves another idol, a more dangerous tyranny; we shall have arrogated to ourselves and to the current generation a truth which is not our possession, but belongs to the whole company of Saints: those from whom we received it, in tradition, and those future generations to whom we shall pass it on in sacred trust.

The bonds that link us, the living, with the dead also ensure that we 'connect' our slender grasp of the truth, however personally real and valid, to the wisdom of the ages. Truth is not usually found by counting votes in synods; though Councils have been called – and rightly called – to pronounce on issues of belief and to establish a common mind. There are times when we find ourselves saying, with the early Apostles, 'it seems good to the Holy Spirit and to us . . . ' Such a time, most certainly, came at Vatican II when the flood-gates opened and brought new hope, fresh possibilities of 'aggiornamento' to all our ailing institutions. But the influence the Council has exerted on a harassed Church and a hungry world came not from the personal authority and undoubted sanctity of Pope John in summoning it; nor from the clarity and wisdom of its various pronouncements; but very largely from the weight of history and tradition that lay behind and impelled it. In the work of this Council, as in that first Council of Jerusalem in Acts 15, was seen the work of the Spirit, setting the Church free to be its true self in and for the world.

It is in the Communion of Saints that the vision of certainty, the action of the Spirit, and the vision of absurdity, our groping grasp of the truth, meet and cohere. Whether we think of them as 'the ancestors', or as those whom Christ has called his friends and extended family, we know we belong to them and to each other in and with them. It is no accident that we speak of 'communion'; our belonging is more than mere membership of a family or a society, bound together by ties of blood or belief. It is rather the organic union which Paul speaks of as limbs in the Body; or John as branches of the Vine. Although, as with other articles of faith, it may be for much of the time just that and no more; still it is an overarching, ever-present reality most keenly experienced when we gather for the Eucharist and recall the presence of those Companions of the Co-inherence, 'the whole company of heaven'.

To celebrate the Communion of Saints is more than a 'commemoration' which we make of All Souls; just as a celebration of the Eucharist is more than a 'commemoration' of Calvary. We honour them, the ones who have reflected the uncreated Light as those myriads of cats' eyes reflect the headlamps and guide us through foggy nights and twisting lanes to our destination: the windows through which we catch the sun's radiance. But in joining our prayer, however imperfect, with theirs we are joining those other friends of Jesus whom he invited to share his vigil. Austin Farrer sums it up for us with his passionate lucidity:

> Where Jesus is, there is the Communion of Saints: his life never lives, his action never acts, alone: he gives his saints everywhere a part of it. Jesus gathered his disciples round him in Gethsemane to pray with him, and they fell asleep. Unsleeping, his saints pray with him in glory, where their whole life becomes a prayer; a holy desire, strong and efficacious, for the fulfilment

of Christ's redemption, and the accomplishment of his kingdom; a perfect union of heart and mind with the society of love . . . [17]

AT PEACE WITH THE PAST

For any one observer of All Saints-tide there must be a hundred who persist year by year in wearing a poppy (red or white) for Remembrance. This, with Christmas and Harvest, continues to be one of the folk festivals still popularly observed. For those who have not taken vows of total abstinence from public worship it is a sign of patriotic 'pietas', solidarity with those who have made the 'supreme sacrifice', to join the British Legion and the uniformed organisations in singing 'O God our Help . . . ' at the local cenotaph. As with other variants of folk religion, Remembrance Sunday can be an excuse for indulging in nostalgia and flag-waving jingoism; it can also provide, even for the vast majority of the population for whom the two World Wars are past history and not personal experience, an opportunity to make an act of recollection, penitence and thanksgiving.

Time was when 'Armistice Day' (as it was called) was celebrated on November 11th and brought the whole nation to a halt for two minutes of silent recollection. In 1919, at the first anniversary of the Armistice, buses and trains halted, passengers alighted and stood heads bowed beside their parked cars; factories ceased production, no surgeons operated and even planes switched off their engines. London seemed like the petrified city of Pompeii. Public opinion demanded an annual commemoration and 'Poppy Day' with its mandatory two minutes' silence, the Last Post at the Whitehall Cenotaph and at local cenotaphs throughout the country, became the day when the nation honoured its slaughtered youth, expressed its corporate grief and said in unison: 'Never Again . . . ' Because we had few occasions to recall the great events in the nation's life (Guy Fawkes, Trafalgar Day, Empire/Commonwealth Day are all partisan, in their different ways, and the last has never caught the imagination), this was adopted as the ritual act to solemnise the best and the worst, the hideous years of courage and carnage.

Since 1945, when the name was changed to 'Remembrance Day' and it was observed on the Sunday nearest the November 11th, its character has gradually changed. Year by year fewer remain with any clear memory of VE or VJ Day, let alone the fields of Flanders. It is not only the young who question its continued observance, its concentration on past events, however historically and emotionally significant, and its meaning at the close of the 20th Century. Owen Chadwick defends it on the grounds that it reminds a secularised society of 'the values of justice and liberty and of yet more, of a realm of spirit which lies under those values.'

> Remembrance [he writes] brought home to men the spirit of compassion, and a feeling for the sufferings of the common people. It also brought home the memory of certain ideals. Not all men died, perhaps, for the ideals for which the politicians said that they should die. But they were real ideals: liberty; respect for weaker peoples; no nation to be exempt from the laws of morality; resolution to prevent war; love of peace as peace was never before loved. The memory of the dead is not only memory of the past. It is also reassertion of values, of infinite moment in a world where the United Nations has already acquired a reputation like that of the League of Nations in its moribund years.[18]

Chadwick's sentiments would have been warmly applauded by G.K. Chesterton who, in his Autobiography, built his account of World War I around the debate conducted by the people of Beaconsfield on the kind of memorial they should erect in 1919. Some (the Practical Party) wanted an amenity – a playing-field for the young, a club for ex-servicemen and their families; others (the Visionary Party) wanted a symbolic Cross or piece of sculpture. The Practical Party won the vote, but the Club was never built. The Visionaries, labelled romantic or superstitious, lost the vote and quietly proceeded to erect a simple Cross by private subscription. There will always be those who wish to convert Remembrance Day into 'Peace Sunday'. This may well happen – indeed the combination of public inertia, the alienation of the young and the dwindling of the British Legion's keenest supporters will force us before long at least to change the pattern of our observance. But, in doing so, some of its special and most emotive characteristics may be lost; and, with them, the power of its symbolism to 'heal the memories'.

Re-membering, the gathering of fragments of the past into the body of the present, is part of what it means to be human. It is also an important constituent of the Judaeo-Christian tradition, from the observance of Passover and the Day of Atonement to the celebration of Easter and Eucharist. When Duff Cooper called his memoirs 'Old Men Forget', he was not denying the particular wisdom of old age which resides in its historical perspective and sense of continuity. 'Old men' remind us of our roots and recall us to the higher purposes for which we exist; beyond economics and the cost of breathing, not submerged beneath youthful arrogance and the illusion that we can live without carrying our history with us. They place us firmly in a tradition which has a past and a future, lest we for one moment forget.

'In times to come, when your son asks you: "What is the meaning of the decrees and laws and customs that Yahweh your God has laid down for you?" you shall tell your son: "Once we were Pharaoh's slaves in Egypt and Yahweh brought us out of Egypt by his mighty hand . . . " (Deuteronomy 6, 20–21). "Remember you were a slave in Egypt" (Deut. 17, 12). And when your son asks in days to come: "What does this mean?" you will tell them . . . "The rite will serve as a sign on your hand would serve . . . " (Exodus 13, 16).' Liberation was tattoed on the hearts and minds of the Jewish people.

This is one aspect of Remembrance which reflects a human need: to dramatise and act out our sense of gratitude and grief (for both are present in this act), loss and deliverance. Ever since the dawn of history this need has been recognised. From the time of Noah and the rainbow, the sign of the Covenant, when he made his sacrifice and expressed his gratitude in the best way he knew; through the history of the Jewish people and their symbolic way of acknowledging their liberation from the powers of darkness and slavery; from Exodus to Holocaust and the establishment of the State of Israel, this has been a mark of identity, national solidarity and religious consciousness. 'Tell them, it is the Lord's Passover' . . . It is not that you were better or more numerous than the Egyptians, but because the Lord had a purpose for his people. Remembrance may thus be seen as our own national Passover and Day of Atonement, when we make peace with the past and acknowledge how far we still have to go if those memories of Hamburg and Hiroshima as well as Blitzkrieg and the Burma Road are to be healed.

For nations, as well as individuals, need to be given an opportunity to grieve. There is not one of us whose family has not suffered bereavement and whose life is not impoverished today by war and the preparations for war. A certain Rabbi Johanan once said: 'The ministering angels wanted to sing a hymn of thanksgiving for the destruction of the Egyptians, but God said, "My children lie drowned in the sea – and you would *sing*?"'[19] If we are not given that opportunity, feelings of pent up anger and aggression, many of them caused by grief, will find expression in acts of violence. A sense of loss – whether personal loss or loss of national status, the security of the Victorian Age and the Edwardian Summers long ago – lies behind the irrational desire for revenge, retaliation, reparation: cries of 'Hang the Kaiser', 'Squeeze them till the pips squeak' after World War I, the cry 'Gotcha!' after the sinking of the Belgrano. They are signs that normally peaceful people wish to express their sense of outrage and frustration: signs of an unhealed, unacknowledged sense of grief. Similarly, behind some of the outbreaks of racial violence, intimidation and 'Paki-bashing' in our inner cities lies the loss of 'Empah', the days of colonial rule, as much as the loss of jobs and of White Anglo-Saxon superiority.

The Psalmists, many of them writing in exile by the waters of Babylon, expressed their own sense of loss – of home, national identity, religious roots – in outbursts of violent language, railing against God as much as their oppressors:

> Destructive daughter of Babel, a blessing on the man who treats you as you have treated us,
> a blessing on him who takes and dashes your babies against the rock!
>
> (Psalm 137)

> God, break their teeth in their mouths,
> wrench out the fangs of these savage lions!
> May they drain away like water running to waste,
> may they wither like trodden grass,

like a slug that melts as it moves,
like an abortion, denied the light of day!

(Psalm 58)

We may be embarassed by such violent language and some would wish to clean up the Bible, itself a violent body of literature, by omitting the Cursing Psalms; the 1928 Prayer Book and the ASB (which bracket them) and the new Roman Office (which omits them) show signs of this sanitising and domesticating process. But there is a danger that the causes of violence will be repressed and a natural expression of grief be overlaid by the platitudes of 'anodyne divines'.

HEALING THE MEMORIES

True, we must point to other ways of resolving conflict. There was a time when we resolved our disputes by duelling pistols, the short, sharp shock of gentlemanly exchange; simple, effective, but no way to end a family feud. Industrial disputes could once be resolved by calling in the militia or the special constables – by lock-outs or simply firing the work-force. Today, for the most part, draconian measures have been replaced by consultation and improved industrial relations. It was once considered inconceivable that 'civilization as we know it' could survive without underpinning and servicing by a slave or helot population. Thanks to a small group of dedicated campaigners and a changed economic climate, slavery was largely abolished and we are left with the abolition of its equivalent in our day: the iniquitous Arms Trade, the economic enslavement of the Third World and the disquietening signs of the emergence of a dispirited and resentful under-class in our inner cities.

To grieve, to 'remember' in penitence and thanksgiving, is never enough. Two young men who fought against each other in the Falklands War lie today buried side by side at Port Stanley. They are commemorated in a poem by the blind Argentinian poet, Jorge Luis Borges:

Each one was Cain and each one Abel – they buried them together.

Caught up in a conflict they could not understand and which remains still unresolved, they serve to remind us that war has still, in Pope John Paul's words, not been removed from the world's agenda; each of us has to add his particular, unique and living stone to the 'Cathedral of Peace' of which he spoke to us. After the grief, the penitence and the thanksgiving there can be no more effective way of 'remembering' the waste and pity of war. In the words of Joe Hill, the 19th Century Trades Union leader: 'Don't mourn, organise!'

After the Act of Remembrance, a prayer enjoins us to 'pledge ourselves anew to the service of God and our fellow men and women; that we may encourage others, and work together for the relief of the needy and for the peace and welfare of the nations.' Just as peace without justice is a lie and a deception, so grieving without self-giving is a mockery and an indulgence. Whether our words become deeds or remain merely hollow cliché and empty rhetoric, so that we lose ourselves in abstractions and a general feeling of benevolence, depends on a willingness to obey the command to 'do good in minute particulars'. In abstract love of humanity, says Dostoevski, one almost always only loves oneself.

At the national/international level this involves looking hard and critically at the sale (by nationalised as well as private industry) of arms and military hardware – worth £3,700 million in 1986, double the amount given in offical Aid – to countries which have to export badly needed food and raw materials to pay for them. It is true that the banning of the sale of arms to oppressive regimes, like Chile or Indonesia, would encourage our competitors to replace them. It is therefore necessary to work simultaneously for genuine arms reduction agreements at an international level. 'If we don't they will' was once an argument used by slavers before Wilberforce: would we refuse to control heroin pushers on the grounds that there will always be others to take their place?

Not only does this 'traffic in death' add to the burden of Third World debt; but it fuels conflicts like the Iran/Iraq war which would have petered out long ago without the unrelenting willingness of the industrialised nations to provide weaponry for both sides. Disarmament, divesting ourselves of arsenals which we increasingly acknowledge we no longer need – and which can only lead to bankruptcy or, worse, to cataclysm and Armageddon – is desirable for itself. But if it means off-loading our discarded weapons-systems on to Third World countries this is only to carry on our East–West conflicts by proxy.[20]

FACING OUR FEARS

At the private and personal level, we have to acknowledge our fears and basic insecurities, the persistence of dualistic stereotypes, inherited prejudices and hardened perceptions of Us and Them. 'Fear not,' says Jesus, 'him that can destroy the body, but fear him that can destroy the soul.' Fear still governs public life and sours international relations; it has dictated every twist of the spiral of the Arms Race – fear of the future, of failure or (worse) of losing prestige and not being taken seriously. It has also bedevilled measures to overcome discrimination against Catholics in N. Ireland: against women, homosexuals and disadvantaged ethnic minorities in our own cities. Fears, both real and false, whereby natural anxiety is manipulated to reinforce the status quo, have to be named and identified. The enemy, like the possibility of reconciliation, lies within.

Remembrance and Reconciliation are two sides of the same coin. It is an affront to the memories of victims of conflict if we make pious pilgrimages to Trafalgar Square or grand gestures at Geneva, but indulge in mutual recrimination, xenophobia or class-war in our own neighbourhood. Instead of bleating about Peace, we should ensure that every Secondary school has a Department of Peace Studies. When a group of Sixth-formers was asked recently what was the most important issue affecting our future, 85% said 'Peace'.

Every parish, synagogue, association or working-men's club should be a centre for some piece of healing or reconciling work. We might well adopt an annual Peace Project, selected on Remembrance Sunday and providing a focus for local support throughout the year; a centre where Jews, Moslems and Christians could learn about and listen to each other; a hospice or home where the dying can be surrounded by love and supported by careful pain-control; a refuge for battered wives, alcoholics or the homeless; a workshop to train black school-leavers or retrain the long-term unemployed. All these are bricks for building together the Cathedral of Peace; particular and continuing signs, like the sign of our Cenotaphs, that we are utterly committed never to 'learn war any more'.

NOTES

1. 'Not like Love, but Love itself': J.A.T. Robinson, 'The Human Face of God', SCM London, 1973, p. 209.
2. Robert Jungk, 'Brighter Than a Thousand Suns', Penguin, 1956, p. 183.
3. Keith Ward, 'The Promise', SPCK London, 1980, p. 3.
4. Kenneth Leech, 'True God', SPCK London, 1985, p. 263.
5. I am quoting (from memory) some remarks made by the Thomist scholar, Tom Berry.
6. Ibid.
7. 'The Environmental Revolution', Hodder London, 1970, pp. 265f., quoted by Hugh Montefiore, 'Can Man Survive?', 1970, p. 46.
8. Quoted by Tim Beaumont, 'Where Shall I Place My Cross?', Hodder London, 1987, p. 85.
9. Letter 151, Sept. 1819, from the Forman Ed, OUP 1948, p. 384.
10. R.M. Rilke, Uncollected Poems, 1906–1926, in 'Selected Works Vol II', Hogarth Press, 1960, tr. J.B. Leishman.
11. Ibid. p. 110, from the Book of Images (1902).
12. Quoted from his Village Sermons by Ronald Jasper, 'Pray Every Day', Collins London, 1976, p. 151.
13. See the Portable North American Indian Reader, ed. F.W. Turner III Penguin, 1977, pp. 252f., 256.
14. Quoted by Geoffrey Parrinder, 'Religion in Africa', Penguin 1969, pp. 85f.
15. This illustration is taken from Gordon Rupp's 'The Sixty Plus', London Collins, 1978, pp. 37 and 42.
16. See especially Leonardo Boff, 'Ecclesio-Genesis – The Base Communities Re-invent the Church', Collins London, 1986, p. 25, where he conceives of the church 'more from the foundation up than from the steeple down. It means accepting the corresponsibility of all in the upbuilding of the church, not just of a limited number belonging to the clerical institution.' As with many feminist theologians, his model of authority is not pyramidal but cyclical.
17. From his sermon, A Share in the Family, in 'A Celebration of Faith', Hodder London, 1970, p. 107.
18. Art. in 'Theology' Vol. LXXIX, Nov. 1976 No. 672, p. 329.
19. Quoted by Victor Gollancz, 'A Year of Grace', Gollancz 1950, p. 34.

20. Two recent encouraging straws in the hitherto discouraging wind of Arms Control:–

1) Colombia and Costa Rica have tabled a resolution on the arms trade to the current 43rd session of the UN asking for a UN register of arms sales, and specifically to 'pursue agreements providing for more openness and transparency on worldwide arms transfers, including the possibility of establishing a system for Member States to report information on arms transfers to the UN.' (Dec. 1988)

2) In the previous month, the Anglican General Synod passed a motion calling upon the British Government to use 'moral rather than commercial criteria to determine policy on arms transfers, especially to areas of Third World conflict.' In the debate, Bishop Richard Harries, chairman of the working party examining 'peacemaking in a nuclear world', made it clear that to their mind 'arms should not be sold or transferred unless there is a compelling moral case to do so.'

Not exactly a Wind of Change – but perhaps a move in the right direction?

Epilogue

I, singularly moved
To love the lovely that are not beloved,
Of all the Seasons, most
Love Winter.

(Coventry Patmore)

In the course of our travels through the landscape of the Christian Year we have tried to relate the specifically Christian seasons and festivals to the underlying cycle of the natural seasons and also to the human cycle of birth, maturation, ageing and death. Unlike Bunyan's 'Puritan Progress' from the City of Destruction to the Celestial Mountains, it has been a more earthly, ecological pilgrimage.

The Christian Year begins with the annual miracle of the irruption of light into the surrounding darkness, when by a happy congruence – or coincidence – Jewish Chanukah and Roman Saturnalia are combined and subsumed within Advent/Christmas. We set off at the year's midnight when the sap is sunk lowest and the dark world waits for the dawn, the coming of the Day-spring.

Yet if His Majesty, our Sovereign Lord,
Should of his own accord
Friendly himself invite,
And say 'I'll be your guest tomorrow night . . .

For all the warning and the waiting, he still catches us off our guard and contantly takes us by surprise.

Christ cannot find a chamber in the inn.
We entertain him always like a stranger,
And, as at first, still lodge him in a manger.[1]

As the Year unfolds and winter gives way to spring, we live through the annual cycle of death and rebirth. The community, also, has to celebrate its 'birth-day'; the Pentecostal tongues of fire warm our hearts while that 'busy old fool, unruly Sun' breaks through to warm the earth. In high summer its radiance is outshone for a few dazzling moments by the 'uncreated Light' of the transfigured Christ. Then, as its powers weaken and the days shorten once more, the fruits of earth are gathered in and stored up with the stocks of winter fuel, the memories and the remembered dead. 'And I saw a new heaven and a new earth . . . I saw the holy city, and the new Jerusalem, coming down from God out of heaven, as beautiful as a bride all dressed for her husband.' All is gathered up, recollected at All Saints-tide and we are ready for a new chapter in the human, natural and liturgical story.

There is a wisdom here that bites deeper than mere knowledge of facts, dogmas or ideologies. Truths are being communicated not in words or concepts, but in shared experience. Each of us is enabled to 'slot in' as and where we can; grasp truths not in a dogmatic, systematic way (how many of us, in fact, learn that way?), but rhythmically, liturgically; allow those truths to seep through the pores of the skin, drip by drip and week by week. If we are subjected, by the Ministry of the Word, to a lifelong process of education or 'edification', it is education not only of the mind but of the imagination and the emotions also.

Here poetry, as we have found, has an important part to play; and particularly, for Judaeo–Christians, the poetry of the Psalms which must have formed a significant part of the religious training of any devout rabbi in the time of Jesus. We know from the Gospel quotations how closely his mind was following Psalm 22 which sustained him through the agony of Crucifixion. We are also aware that his image of the Good Shepherd draws directly from the 23rd Psalm.

It is not so widely acknowledged that that beloved 'Song for All Seasons', which serves as well to comfort the bereaved as to send newly wedded couples on their way, has its own narrative shape and tells its own story of a year's cycle. Whether or no the author be David himself, it is clearly someone who knows the ways of sheep and shepherds and understands the hazards of a pastoral life-style that is far from idyllic. It is told from the point of view of the sheep, not the shepherd: Dominus regit me – God, who has the whole world in his hands, holds me in his providential care and will not let me go.[2]

The poem opens with the Spring and finds the flock grazing in the lowlands where the dew lies heavy on the grass. The shepherd knows where the best pasture is to be found; but he also knows the dangers of over-grazing when the pasture cannot sustain the pressure of numbers: erosion threatens, the water is polluted, the sheep weaken and are attacked by liver-fluke. If the flock is to grow and be properly nourished it needs fresh pastures. So, as the season moves on, the flock moves with it, up the valley to the higher ground. This may spell danger; the shepherd may need his 'rod and staff' to beat off snakes or to prod (i.e. 'convert' stragglers and deviants back on to the right path (it is Murphy's Law that if there is a wrong path sheep will surely take it). A 'cast' sheep may need turning over, the brambles and ditches have to be negotiated.

Possibly not all will arrive at the higher ground. The 'vale of soul-making' may well prove 'the valley of the shadow of death'. The hungry hawk and other predators, even rustlers, lie in wait for the unwary. But once arrived on the 'mesa', the highlands or 'table', the air is good and the pastures fresh. Even so, summer will bring its own problems: infesting flies and tics to 'trouble' and torment. The shepherd needs oil for embrocation, but also to apply to the horns; sheep can be quarrelsome creatures and when they rut the horns can become locked. Oil ensures that the heads and horns can be easily disentangled.

It is, however, a time of peace and great contentment. As summer declines into autumn, the flies recede and it is a period of gentle grazing, building up strength for the winter – the cup is full to overflowing. The flock can be left while the harvest below is being gathered. But not for long. Storms are expected and they will soon have to descend, leaving behind them pasture well fertilized by nitrates, the 'goodness and mercy' that must provide for others and for next year. It is a time for going home, down to the valleys for winter and the conclusion of the cycle. They return to the sheepfold for protection and for lambing: not the 'house' of bricks and mortar, but the 'shekinah', the nearness and overshadowing presence of God. The poet of Psalm 23 knows his theology as well as his zoology and for him, as for William Blake, 'eternity is in love with the productions of time'.

With the insights drawn from life-experience he makes the leap of faith that Jahweh, the sky-god, is his personal guardian and guide: 'My Shepherd'. He who holds the whole world in his hands holds me – the hairs of my head are all numbered. Whatever happens, through the 'changes and chances of this fleeting world', through the valley of the shadow, he will not let go if I stick near to him, from spring right through to winter and beyond.

It requires of me more than an act of faith: it requires me to entertain hope, the virtue today that is 'rarer than radium'. It is a spring virtue; no blind, bland deceiver, but rooted in reality and the raw deed of Easter Resurrection. It has seen many winters come and go and knows that if winter comes spring cannot be far behind. It knows there is light at the end of the tunnel; there are signals if I open my eyes to them. Expect nothing and I am likely to see nothing: expect anything and I am likely to be surprised. Hope, as the poet Norman Nicholson once said, is a theological virtue, but a geological grace.

But if experience has brought the confidence to hope it also warns against any indulging in false hopes. Keats' 'lusty Spring' and luxurious Summer of rumination on 'the honied cud of youthful thought' say more about the leisured and privileged classes of the Regency era than about our angst-ridden, post-industrial age. It may be, as some wit remarked, that 'nostalgia isn't what it was'; but by focussing our minds on the Good Old Days ('Where are the snows of yesteryear?') it can feed our selective and unhistorical imaginations. History reminds me that Keats' 'lusty Spring' and those magical Edwardian Summers were enjoyed by a leisured few on the profits of the Slave Trade and at hideous cost to the victims of Victorian industrialism. It is the function of hope to rescue us both from despair of the present and from dangerous day-dreams about the past. Nostalgia only weakens it and blinds us to the infinite possibilities of the future.

It is possible to think of ourselves as living the whole cycle of the year's seasons not just once, but every day of our lives. The 23rd Psalm can be interpreted as the story of a single day in the life of Everyman/woman as much as the story of a single year. We set off in the spring-tide of hope and expectancy, ready to voyage to the end of the world, if need be, for a lost or worthy cause. Midday brings a summer sluggishness, the need for a break and a breather. There have been some knocks and setbacks as well as successes in the morning stint; there is still time, if we fight off inertia, to recoup our losses, re-focus and prepare for the next stint. In my life's afternoon I may find quite a different job to the one that filled my morning. Midday, mid-career, like the summer, is a good time for reflection and certainly for changing gear.

The evening is the autumn of my day: more relaxed and possibly also more creative. The things I had no time for in my ambitious spring and summer I have time for now. Time to think, time for my family, neglected godchildren and eagerly awaited grandchildren: time for a drink and an unhurried evening with friends: time to exercise the muscles I never used at work, to learn new skills or mend old furniture: time to pray for those who have no time or energy to pray for themselves. I may tire more easily, perhaps, but it is a positive weariness, not a negative world-weariness that comes from standing still. In the evening the world seems a saner place to live in as the pace slows down. The colours quieter and more subtle than in the garish sun.

My day is slowly moving into night. I may dread it as the winter of my discontent, the sweats and nightmares that waken me at 3 a.m., that deep midwinter of the human spirit. Or I may (as I expect Coventry Patmore did) look forward to it as a time of peace, rest and refreshment. Every mile is two in winter, says George Herbert; and that is true of old age – everything takes more energy than we seem to have. So we must change pace, walk more slowly: be gentle and patient with ourselves, which some find harder than being patient with other people.

And of course there may be pain, always worst at night with nothing to distract you.

> November's sky is chill and drear,
> November's leaf is red and sere.

Age brings creaking joints like rusty gates; and winter can be pitiless to the old. The night hours can stretch out endlessly, bringing loneliness and the ghostly haunting of nameless fears.

But at least you know that morning is at hand – 'heaviness may endure for a night, but joy cometh in the morning'. It is this knowledge, which is also an act of faith born of experience, that keeps us going in the small hours before the dawn, in that eerie half-light when the body's resistance is at its lowest.

Living this cycle of the seasons every day of our lives takes away all fear of my own life's winter. I see the cycle imprinted on the day, the year, the very earth and all creation. It is the cycle of dying and rising again, losing and finding; I know it is an act of faith that day will follow night and spring will follow winter. But it is faith rooted in my historical memory, in my observation of the way things are and must be.

To that extent I confess myself, like Albert Camus, a 'winter Christian'. When times are hard and the frosts are biting it becomes more, not less necessary to believe. And at this point God meets us, as he met Dietrich Bonhoeffer in his Gestapo gaol:

> God goeth to every man when sore bestead,
> Feedeth body and spirit with his bread,
> For Christians, heathens alike he hangeth dead:
> And both alike forgiving.

Then, on New Year's Day, 1945, four months before his execution he prays:

> With every power for good to stay and guide me,
> comforted and inspired beyond all fear,
> I'll live these days with you in thought beside me,
> and pass, with you, into the coming year.[3]

It is as if he heard, in the distance, those familiar words: 'Lo, the winter is past, the rain is over and gone; the flowers appear on the earth; the time of the singing of birds is come, and the voice of the turtle is heard in our land.'

NOTES

1. The full text of this beautiful anonymous poem is to be found in the Oxford Book of English Verse (Quiller-Couch ed.) 1939, No. 69, p. 95.
2. For many of the insights that follow I am indebted to the interpretation of Psalm 23 by Philip Keller, himself a shepherd, brought up with the herdsmen of E. Africa. (Zondervan, U.S.A., 1970)
3. D. Bonhoeffer, Letters and Papers from Prison, Collins Fontana, 1959, p. 174.

Index to Main Topics

Index of Names